Young Adult Library Services

Young Adult Library Services

Challenges and Opportunities

Edited by

Anthony Bernier and Shari Lee

ROWMAN & LITTLEFIELD
Lanham • Boulder • New York • London

Published by Rowman & Littlefield
An imprint of The Rowman & Littlefield Publishing Group, Inc.
4501 Forbes Boulevard, Suite 200, Lanham, Maryland 20706
www.rowman.com

86-90 Paul Street, London EC2A 4NE

British Library Cataloguing in Publication Information Available

Library of Congress Cataloging-in-Publication Data

Names: Bernier, Anthony, editor. | Lee, Shari, 1958- editor.
Title: Young adult library services : challenges and opportunities / edited
  by Anthony Bernier and Shari Lee.
Description: Lanham : Lexington Books 2024. | Includes bibliographical
  references and index. | Summary: "Finally, a single-volume
  comprehensively introducing and addressing the most pressing issues and
  opportunities in YA services. Edited by two senior YA scholars, Young
  Adult Library Services: Challenges and Opportunities will solve the
  problem of cobbling together disparate readings into one efficient
  treatment for a YA services textbook"—Provided by publisher.
Identifiers: LCCN 2023051456 (print) | LCCN 2023051457 (ebook) | ISBN
  9781538179284 (cloth) | ISBN 9781538179291 (paperback) | ISBN
  9781538179307 (epub)
Subjects: LCSH: Young adults' libraries—Administration. | Libraries and
  teenagers. | Young adults' libraries—United States—Administration. |
  Libraries and teenagers—United States. | Young adults'
  libraries—Collection development. | Internet in young adults'
  libraries.
Classification: LCC Z718.5 .Y6565 2024 (print) | LCC Z718.5 (ebook)
LC record available at https://lccn.loc.gov/2023051456
LC ebook record available at https://lccn.loc.gov/2023051457

♾™ The paper used in this publication meets the minimum requirements of American
National Standard for Information Sciences—Permanence of Paper for Printed Library
Materials, ANSI/NISO Z39.48-1992.

Contents

Part Three: Institutional Capacities and Models

Acknowledgments

The editors would like to thank and acknowledge the efforts of library and information science graduate student assistants Kassandra Dineen (San Jose State University iSchool) and Camryn Duff (St. John's University, Division of Library and Information Science [DLIS]), who not only helped with the production phases of this project but also provided substantial conceptual contributions. Jointly, they kept the focus on issues that students felt were important rather than simply those the authors prioritized. The project was also aided by Edgar Moza, St. John's DLIS student Dr. Elizabeth Macaluso, and St. John's DLIS youth services adjuncts Gabrielle Hew and Christopher Stewart.

More broadly, each of the editors would like to "shout out" the students appearing in our own young adult classes. Semester after semester and year after year, they rely on us to prepare them not only for the ever-challenging job market but also for the insights and skills they need to progressively serve young adults through libraries during uncertain times. These are the needs *Young Adult Library Services: Challenges and Opportunities* attempts to address.

Finally, the editors would like to thank our publisher, Charles Harmon, at Rowman & Littlefield for helping us bring this volume to the field. May the profession one day better acknowledge his long-standing contributions to library science.

Introduction to Young Adult Library Services: Challenges and Opportunities

What appears between the covers of this book could well be considered an entire master class in young adult library services. Indeed, these essays comprise the only such collection dedicated to preparing young adult librarians to deliver professional-level services for and with young adults.

Young Adult Library Services: Challenges and Opportunities is edited and written by two distinguished and senior youth services scholars with contributions from a select group of highly qualified and experienced youth services scholars and practitioners as well as the unique perspectives of library and information science (LIS) graduate students. The work represents the most comprehensive treatment of challenges and opportunities the field has yet produced on serving this otherwise institutionally and historically marginalized user population.

Contributors were selected based on their respective areas of scholarly expertise and distinguished records of direct practice in young adult services. They were asked to focus on challenges that they believe are most at issue in the field and were further tasked with identifying opportunities for where and how these could be addressed.

Each of the two editors reviewed and provided feedback on every draft, as did at least two Master of Library and Information Science (MLIS) graduate student assistants. Upon receiving the revised manuscripts, the editors, together with student assistants, developed follow-up questions for each essay intended to spark further classroom discussion and assignments.

While the range and depth of issues covered attempt to address today's most pressing, challenging, and complex concerns facing LIS scholars, instructors, students, practitioners, and the field more broadly, no collection can anticipate or address every concern, and of course, more arise every day. However, by engaging with these essays (individually and especially collectively) and exploring the discussion questions provided, students and professionals at all levels will gain increased topical confidence and a broader critical understanding of what professional-grade young adult services could mean for today's libraries.

The chapters are presented in three sections that focus, respectively, on young adult programs and services, intellectual freedom and collections, and institutional capacities and models. The chapters in part I promote and encourage the use of popular culture, social media, program management, and social services to improve library services to teens.

Part II delves into the challenges and opportunities with which information professionals must contend in today's fast evolving technological and politically charged environments. Topics covered in this section include collection development, self-censorship, book banning, misinformation, defining the "new" teen, and serving the LGBTQ+ teen community.

Part III is concerned with the collective abilities, resources, and organizational structures that ensure the institution's capacity to provide quality programs and services while adapting to new challenges and opportunities. Topics in this section contend with managing up; the historical and contemporary challenges that face public and school libraries; the challenges of creating the first teen space; filling the void left by the now defunct magazine *Voice of Youth Advocates*; young adult services as developmental work; organizing a youth services unit using vertical or horizontal integration; and race, racism, and whiteness in school library programs.

These three parts offer a comprehensive exploration of key aspects in the field, ranging from innovative program development and intellectual freedom considerations to the foundational institutional capacities that underpin effective young adult service delivery. Nevertheless, these essays should not be interpreted as the "last word" on the service challenges they respectively and collectively articulate. This is where the benefit of the discussion questions can be realized, as they will help open up critical thinking, thoughtful dialogue, and analysis and spark innovation and experimentation.

In attempting to provide public value to the dynamic and diverse populations that young people present to libraries, innovation and experimentation should be considered core professional competencies. And given the cultural, political, environmental, and even epidemiological uncertainties young people face, libraries owe them nothing less.

WHY IS THIS BOOK NEEDED?

It's no secret that young adult services live in the "way back seat" of library and information science. Ever in the shadow of service to children and historically riven in fractious relationships between public and school libraries, service to young adults perpetually suffers varying types of inadequacies and inequities. Consequently, young adult services remain compromised in their capacity to build institutional or professional influence and to grow and develop beyond ritual, repetition, and even "superstition," as was argued over 35 years ago (Edmonds, 1987).

Another consequence of being professionally marginalized is that young adult services has yet to produce a coherent and comprehensive textbook to meaningfully cohere, support, and prepare practitioners to connect library value with young people. Instead, LIS instructors commonly cobble together what few evidence-based articles scholars produce along with largely non-evidence–based practitioner publications (Bernier, 2019). These problems are compounded when "youth courses" purporting to "cover" both children and young adult domains frequently shortchange professional engagement with the latter or focus too narrowly on materials.

These pedagogical liabilities structurally inhibit the development and advancement of the field and condemn young adult services to perpetually pedestrian positions.

Young Adult Library Services: Challenges and Opportunities begins to address this long-standing and institutional inequity in preparing professionals.

In this one volume, youth services faculty and instructors will find essential, single, broad, and diverse engagement with scholars and acknowledged experts on the most pressing challenges confronting young adult services today. Students at both the graduate and undergraduate levels will appreciate field-tested topics delivered through accessible treatments. Practicing young adult (and "youth") librarians will appreciate the support and evidence-based analysis they failed to receive while earning their master's degrees. Earnest young adult advocates will value the pursuit of issues beyond pedestrian cliché and perpetual entry-level conversations. And instructors and students alike will appreciate the brevity of concisely focused chapters and discussion questions.

REFERENCES

Bernier, A. (2019, April). Isn't it time for youth services instruction to grow up? Superstition or scholarship. *Journal of Education for Library and Information Science, 60*(2), 118–38.

Edmonds, L. M. (1987). From superstition to science: The role of research in strengthening public library services to children. *Library Trends, 35*(3), 509–20.

Part One

Young Adult Programs and Services

1

Using Popular Culture to Connect Teens and Public Libraries

Shari Lee

The disconnect between teens and public libraries has been well documented and is one reason teens over the past two decades have reported that they find library services unsatisfactory and the library unwelcoming, uninviting, or un-cool (Jones, 2002; Campos, 2020). Balancing teens' expectations of librarians with the reality that librarians are people, too, could foster better relationships between libraries and teens; however, being responsive to their needs would likely prove a better strategy. Paying attention to the trends and popular culture that teens value, consume, and create would only further this objective and result in higher-quality library experiences for teens.

Ignoring or dismissing the trends and popular culture that teens value, create, and consume as insignificant, unserious, or ridiculous sends a message to teens that they are likely similarly perceived. On the contrary, gaining an understanding of, and even appreciation for, these aspects of teen culture would provide infinite opportunities for communication, comradery, and sharing (i.e., connection). As such, the value of popular culture as a tool in efforts to eliminate barriers to teen services is worth, at the very least, exploring. The dearth of research on popular culture in library and information science (LIS) requires, however, that we draw on research from other disciplines to better understand this value. Jeffery Passe (2002) argues that

> [a]s educators, we need to know what our students are watching. If we wish to understand their references, their role models and anti-role models—indeed, if

we want to know what makes our students tick—we have to be in touch with the popular culture that influences them. (para. 3)

Young adult librarians must also contend with the impact of popular culture on the lives of the young people with whom they aim to engage. This thinking aligns well with Morrell (2002), who says that the arguments for the inclusion of popular culture in traditional educational curricula are persuasive and have generated both excitement and trepidation among urban educators. Drawing on his experiences as an educator and teacher trainer, Morrell (2002) finds that many of his colleagues have expressed support for integrating popular culture into their classes but also admit to feeling unprepared and overwhelmed by the prospect. Much of the uncertainty and confusion surrounding the incorporation of popular culture into education, he finds, arises from a lack of understanding.

So, what is popular culture? The abbreviation "pop" (as in music) goes back to the late 1950s, but the term "pop culture" did not become mainstream until the 1980s. Generally, pop culture is recognized as the people's culture—the culture that predominates in a society at a point in time (Delaney, 2007, para. 1). However, the answer usually depends on who's doing the defining, as context always matters when considering pop culture. John Storey (2015), for example, presents six definitions, which provide varying and broad perspectives on what popular culture encompasses. Two of the most relevant to our cause are discussed below.

The first states that "[p]op culture is a culture that is widely favored or well-liked by many" (Storey, 2015, p. 5). In this perspective, popular culture is seen as cultural expressions and artifacts that enjoy widespread acceptance and popularity among a broad range of people. It is marked by its appeal to the general public and its ability to resonate with a large audience. In the second, "Pop culture is whatever is left after we subtract what we decide is *high culture*" (Storey, 2015, p. 5). This definition suggests that popular culture emerges as what remains when we remove the concept of *high culture* from the cultural landscape. In other words, it encompasses cultural elements that are not typically associated with elite or refined artistic expressions (i.e., *low culture*).

Overall, Storey's six definitions provide a multifaceted understanding of popular culture, highlighting its ubiquity, relationship to commercial interests, connection to folk practices, negotiation of power dynamics, and the sometimes-blurred line between authenticity and commercialization. These perspectives collectively emphasize the complexity and diverse nature of popular culture as it interacts with society and shapes cultural identity. What these definitions share, Storey (2015) concludes, "is the insistence that whatever else popular culture might be, it is definitely a culture that only emerged following industrialization and urbanization" (p. 12).

This can be seen in Victorian-era Britain (1820–1914), where the first Industrial Revolution (1760–1830) spurred a growth in capitalism and social change that included an upsurge in leisure spending and leisure activities, which directly drove the rise of popular culture. Anderson (2016) notes that increased literacy rates within the working class (who had been taught to read in state-funded schools), along with the technology for large-scale distribution, also led to the development of a market for cheap popular literature. This growing demand, in turn, led to the publication of the first penny dreadfuls. Also known by the equally pejorative alternatives "penny awfuls" and "penny bloods," these were literary serials, 8 to 16 pages in length, which were published in weekly installments for the very affordable price of a penny. For comparison, Charles Dickens's serials raked in a shilling (i.e., 12 pennies) per installment during the same period.

In her investigation of the nature of the penny dreadful, Anderson (2016) finds that these serials were initially aimed at all ages of the newly literate working class (pejoratively "the unwashed"), but the target audience later shifted toward working-class young men. The subjects of these stories were usually detective, criminal, or sensational horror and gore, featuring characters such as Sweeney Todd. Penny dreadfuls not only developed a reputation for being scandalous, but in the words of George A. Sala (1862), himself an early consumer and later a contributor to this genre of fiction, penny dreadfuls also offered access to

> a world of dormant peerages, of murderous baronets, and ladies of title addicted to the study of toxicology, of gypsies and brigand-chiefs, men with masks and women with daggers, of stolen children, withered hags, heartless gamesters, nefarious roués, foreign princesses, Jesuit fathers, gravediggers, resurrection-men, lunatics and ghosts. (p. 148)

"The great unwashed had been taught how to read, the argument went, but not what to read" (Anderson, 2016, para. 9). The first penny serial was published in the 1830s. By the 1850s, there were approximately 100 penny-fiction publishers with more than a million juvenile periodicals sold every week. The penny dreadful was indeed "a 19th-Century British publishing phenomenon" (Anderson, 2016, para. 9). These publications were

> Britain's first taste of mass-produced popular culture for the young, and—like movies, comics, video games and computer games in the century that followed—was held responsible for anything from petty theft to homicide. (Summerscale, 2016, para. 3)

Sound familiar? As Anderson (2016) puts it, "these far-fetched tales of intrigue and adventure were the video nasties or shoot 'em up games of their age, and were held responsible for real-life acts of criminality and bloodshed" (para. 3).

A similar parallel can be drawn from the response to the death of Sir Arthur Conan Doyle's much beloved character, Sherlock Holmes, who rolled off the pages of *The Strand* magazine and into the hearts of the British people in 1887. Frustrated with the character's popularity, which he felt eclipsed his more serious work, Conan Doyle made the decision to kill off the character he had come to detest. He committed the deed in 1893. In her analysis of the uproar the detective's death triggered, Armstrong (2016) surmises that Conan Doyle likely thought "Holmes was dead, and that was that," but he didn't entirely understand fans, especially Sherlock Holmes' fans. She finds that the public backlash was unlike anything that had been previously seen in response to a fictional event. More than 20,000 *Strand* magazine subscribers canceled their subscriptions in protest. This was such a huge blow to the magazine that the staff referred to the detective's death as *the dreadful event*. "Outraged fans wrote to the magazine in protest: *You brute!* one letter addressed to Conan Doyle began. Americans started *Let's Keep Holmes Alive* clubs. In spite of the protests, Conan Doyle stuck to his guns, calling Holmes' death *justifiable homicide*" (Armstrong, 2016, para. 4).

These historical examples show that some aspects of pop culture did, in fact, emerge nearly two centuries ago and are not recent developments. Specifically, fan culture existed well before the internet, and some aspects have prevailed across decades; the passion today's teens have for the pop culture they value is not unique to our time; and society's strained relationship with youth and the popular culture they consume existed well before adolescence was identified as a separate (and problematic) stage of human development. Most importantly, we see that pop culture is, and has always been, driven by young people.

In fact, trend-setting teens have always been the most sought-after market segment *because* they determine what is cool. This means that a certain level of trend watching is required if one is to engage with teen popular culture. Yes, trend watching is a thing! Before the internet, marketing companies actually employed researchers (aka "cool hunters") to understand these teens and, therefore, the trends (i.e., what was cool). They would then market this knowledge back to teens until it became a part of the mainstream teen consumer market/culture, but, by then, it would no longer be cool. So the process would begin again.

The internet, and social media more specifically, made it possible for teens to reach out and share, like, dislike, and follow, thus making it much easier for these companies to learn. The information they once spent a small fortune gathering is now handed to them—for free. Essentially, teens have now become a part of the marketing machine primarily because of social media. Teen culture went from marketers following teens around in an effort to learn what was cool to teens using social media to tell their peers, and therefore, the world and marketing companies, what they like/dislike, which then determines what is popular and therefore, what is cool.

This supports the idea that trend watching is viable, even necessary, when aiming to keep up with popular culture. Fortunately, there are many online options available that can be helpful in this endeavor. These include trend-tracking websites (e.g., Trend Hunter and Google Trends); podcasts (e.g., NPR's "It's Been a Minute," "Nerdette," and "Pop Culture Happy Hour" and Apple's "Homophilia"); YouTube channels (e.g., React, StudioJake Media, and Geeks + Gamers); blogs and websites that cater specifically to teens (e.g., Teen Vogue, Seventeen, Teen Ink, and Buzzfeed's Quizzes); social media platforms, where following relevant hashtags and accounts can provide an insider perspective of teen pop culture trends, interests, and discussions (e.g., Instagram, TikTok, and Snapchat) as well as the book review algorithms within these platforms that are popular with teens (e.g., Bookstagram, BookTube, and BookTok[1]); and streaming platforms that cater to teen audiences, which can provide knowledge of the TV shows, series, and movies teens are watching and offer insight into their interests (e.g., Netflix, Hulu, Disney+, and Max). However, one must keep in mind that teen pop culture trends evolve rapidly, so staying flexible and open to new platforms and methods is essential if pop culture is to be effectively used to connect with teens.

What is the value of pop culture to young adult library services specifically? When looking at libraries and young adult literature, for example, Veit and Osada (2010) argue that they were ill-prepared to adequately provide readers' advisory to teens when they first entered the field. They found that teens were neither impressed nor interested in reading the titles they loved when they were in graduate school; they were even less impressed with the award-winning titles, which were the primary focus in their coursework. Instead, teen preferences were profoundly influenced by their peers' reading choices as well as popular trends. Milliot (2014) similarly observes that "the importance of movies to book-buying habits cannot be overstated. Teens reported that among the most important factors that made them aware of particular titles involved either seeing a movie based on a book or having seen a book trailer at a movie theater" (para. 9). Even so, the young adult librarians are quick to point out that they are not

> advocating for a complete overhaul of young adult literature syllabi, either—on the whole, they are thoughtful and thorough—but given the relevance of these books to real teens, even guiding library students toward bestseller lists to choose some of their required reading would be a powerful step in opening students' eyes to what books—and what types of books—are popular. LIS literature courses can retain their strong teaching of critical thinking and library theory while still broadening the scope just a little wider to include popular literature. (Veit & Osada, 2010, p. 12)

It must be emphasized that since the publication of this article, there have been numerous instances of young adult librarians using pop culture to connect with, and better serve, teens. The question is, have library schools made this shift? Unfortunately, the lack of standardization across youth services courses makes this a difficult question to answer. What *is* known is that the disconnect endures.

In any event, the approach Veit and Osada (2010) propose regarding young adult literature would work well when considering the use of other aspects of pop culture to connect with teens. The overarching goal would be to understand the relationship between the mass media that informs today's pop culture (e.g., social media trends and memes, TV/streaming platforms, radio/podcasts, newspapers, and magazines) and aspects of teen popular culture (e.g., music, sports, video games, comics, fandoms/fanworks, food, slang/greetings, movies, videos, and TV shows/series).

An understanding of how these are connected is also beneficial because there was a time, not so long ago, when these were considered and treated as separate aspects or components of popular culture—a time when one didn't necessarily affect the others. Today, they are connected, as never before, through the internet and social media specifically. As many have observed, we are no longer tied to time and place (or space) when it comes to the pop culture we consume and create. We stream everything; we consume books, magazines, and newspapers on a variety of mobile devices; competitive gaming has become a viral sensation; technology has democratized music production; and traditional sports organizations have incorporated esports into their portfolios. We are constantly connected.

So how do we use this knowledge to connect with teen library users? Get to know the teens in your community and invite them to get to know you. Tap into teen pop culture and trends. Trend watch! Get to know what these teens consume, create, and value—as well as what the varying age groups read, watch, listen to, and play. Read reviews of this content. Invite teen users and the teen advisory board (TAB) to make selections for the collection and share pop culture–themed programming ideas. Create a hackerspace or breakerspace. Provide access to mobile devices for teen users. Know their technology preferences/usage and keep up with social media platforms they use—and use these platforms to reach teens. Authenticity is crucial when interacting with teens, but this should not be an issue once you get to know your teens and your efforts are sincere.

Explore different but related formats of popular works, such as Sherlock Holmes. Today, as we stand at the dawn of the fourth industrial revolution, the canon boasts 4 novels and 56 short stories, and 75 actors have played Holmes in more than 200 movies. There have been TV adaptations, several series, and one of the oldest and most active fandoms, which continues to produce a plethora of fanfiction and fanworks (content created in honor of a canon)—fanart, fanmixes, fanvids, meta, cosplay, and even Holmes-themed tea. When we understand what all the fuss is about, connecting with teens will always be less of a challenge.

As noted on one pop culture blog, to understand pop culture, you must engage with it (Pageplots.com, 2023). So, they aver, try something new—like gaming! Not brave enough? How about a new fashion trend instead? See the latest "it" group/singer or catch a "hot" Broadway production. You have nothing to lose, and you might even broaden your perspective on some aspects of pop culture. Stay open minded! Everyone has different preferences when it comes to pop culture, so there might be aspects that you dislike or even loathe. But before dismissing something outright, try stepping back and taking a more objective approach. Pop culture comprises much that is deemed good, questionable, and even bad; you don't have to like it all. It's okay to dislike something, but understanding why, as well as why others might enjoy it, can lead to a shift in thinking. Most of all, be fearless. Pop culture is not for the faint of heart!

DISCUSSION QUESTIONS

- For a job interview question, what one or two sources of youth pop culture would you cite as evidence of keeping current?
- What *professional* sources of information do you find helpful when trying to remain current with youth pop culture?
- How might you address criticism of the inclusion of youth pop culture sources in the library as being dangerous to or damaging to young people?

NOTE

1. Teens/Gen Z are the driving force behind BookTok. It is their preferred platform for creating/consuming young adult book reviews and recommendations—sparking an increase in, and renewed love of, reading in teens. Its major influence on book sales and putting/keeping books on bestseller lists has deemed it a game changer for publishing, when other platforms, such as Bookstagram and BookTube have not had the same impact—not even close. Books reviewed/discussed on BookTok are provided their own tables at Barnes & Noble and are picked up by major publishers. For example, one title from 2018, *They Both Die at the End*, by Adam Silvera, benefited from promotion on BookTok, selling over 680,000 copies!

REFERENCES

Anderson, H. (2016, May). The shocking tale of the penny dreadful. *BBC*. https://www.bbc.com/culture/article/20160502-the-shocking-tale-of-the-penny-dreadful

Armstrong, J. K. (2016, January). How Sherlock Holmes changed the world. *BBC*. https://www.bbc.com/culture/article/20160106-how-sherlock-holmes-changed-the-world

Campos, L. (2020). Eliminating barriers: Building stronger relationships with teen library patrons. *The Serials Librarian*, 79(1-2), 49-56.

Delaney, T. (2007, November/December). Pop culture: An overview. *Philosophy Now: A Magazine of Ideas.* https://philosophynow.org/issues/64/Pop_Culture_An_Overview.

Jones, P. (2002). *New directions for library service to young adults.* American Library Association.

Milliot, J. (2014, February). Children's books: A shifting market: The rise of e-books is one factor affecting book buying in the category. *Publisher's Weekly.* https://www.publishersweekly.com/pw/by-topic/childrens/childrens-industry-news/article/61167-children-s-books-a-shifting-market.html.

Morrell, E. (2002). Toward a critical pedagogy of popular culture: Literacy development among urban youth. *Journal of Adolescent and Adult Literacy, 46*(1), 72–77.

Pageplots.com. (2023, January 30). *What does it mean to be a pop culture expert?* https://pagesplots.com/what-does-it-mean-to-be-a-pop-culture-expert.

Passe, J. (2002). Like it or not: Social educators must keep up with popular culture. *Social Education, 66*(4), 234. https://link.gale.com/apps/doc/A87508012/AONE?u=nysl_oweb&sid=googleScholar&xid=571da359.

Sala, G. A. (1862). *The seven sons of mammon* (Vol. 1). TOHP Burnham.

Storey, J. (2015). *Cultural theory and popular culture: An introduction* (7th ed.). Routledge/Taylor and Francis Group.

Summerscale, K. (2016, April). Penny dreadfuls: The Victorian equivalent of video games. *The Guardian.* https://www.theguardian.com/books/2016/apr/30/penny-dreadfuls-victorian-equivalent-video-games-kate-summerscale-wicked-boy.

Veit, F., & Osada, F. (2010, Summer). Absolutely true experiences of two new librarians: The importance of popular literature in educating young adult librarians. *Young Adult Library Services, 8*(4), 11–13.

2

Open in Different Ways

THE USE OF DISCORD TO RESOLVE TEEN SERVICES CHALLENGES
RESULTING FROM COVID SHUTDOWN (AND THE ACCIDENTAL
CREATION OF A NEW SERVICE)

Jennifer Velásquez

INTRODUCTION

The use of Discord, a popular online communication/sharing platform, offered libraries the opportunity to provide teen activities and social connection during the COVID shutdown, ultimately manifesting as an important, sustainable venue for teen library services.

When employed as a service platform, Discord effectively mitigates the inherent functional barriers present in traditional in-person teen programming (referred to as "activities" throughout this essay). Using the San Antonio Public Library's Discord account, @210teenlibrary, as a backdrop for examination provided an opportunity to consider obvious, but often overlooked, differences between planning approaches for children/tween activities and teen activities. In retrospect, the online delivery method paradoxically revealed universal strengths and flaws pervasive in "in-person" teen activity planning approaches employed by many libraries, which may help refine overall teen service goals. Ultimately, the initial challenge, to keep the library experience "open" while the building was physically shut down, became essential to resolving more elemental challenges (making the library "present" in new ways while open).

DISCORD SERVER @210TEENLIBRARY

When the physical locations of the San Antonio Public Library System were closed due to COVID, the teen services team, at the suggestion of teen users, swiftly set up a Discord server. The server maintained communication between teens and their peers as well as communication between teens and library staff. The initial goal was to limit social isolation, offer information about the library closure, and provide continuity for an established community of "library" teens.

The @210teenlibrary Discord server grew throughout the pandemic, expanding from an inaugural core user group of 11 teens (in May 2020) to an active user group ballooning into the hundreds. Of these teens, 25 percent reported they had never used the physical library before connecting with the library through the server. Teen moderators ran special interest clubs, and conversations took place 24/7. Teens ate lunch and took study breaks together on the server throughout their virtual school days. They said good morning and good night to each other. Teens shared artwork, poetry, memes, and photos of pets and food. They told jokes in the middle of the night and talked about their feelings. Teens wanted reassurances from staff that the server would live on after the pandemic.

Now, long after physical locations have reopened for in-person services, the @210teenlibrary Discord server remains a vibrant virtual "teen branch library"—a branch that never closes. The library system has committed to the server by dedicating a teen services staff work group of six and modest funding for an upgraded Discord platform.

Delving into the details of the @210teenlibrary Discord server and its variety of teen-created and -moderated channels and clubs may cause a not uncommon "make-ours-look-like-yours" library service reaction. Yours should not look like ours because ours has relevance only to our particular group of teens at a given point in time. However, the general service patterns observed throughout these challenging circumstances and the resulting opportunities they offer can help librarians crystalize and extend the notion of what it means to provide activities for teens in the library, whether in a virtual or physical setting.

The specifics of Discord, its unique characteristics and mechanics, are not the things to dwell upon here. Discord will likely be replaced by the next new thing. So when considering the notion of virtual teen activities, let the platform disappear and consider "the why," the goal of its use, rather than "the what" of its features. By doing this, the resulting examination offers insight into the fundamental substance of teen participation and service.

THE SCRAMBLE TO DO SOMETHING

The COVID shutdown saw public libraries, as their physical spaces closed, race to continue serving the public. Libraries were gripped with the desire to do something. Some library services translated well into virtual venues, and some did not. Digital collections, where available, provided connection to the library. Services such as prerecorded YouTube story times for children sprang up across the internet. Virtual story-time programming, just as its in-person counterpart, were low-hanging fruit: A dedicated group of constituents (parents) could be contacted via established means (Facebook) to provide an easily "virtualized" service (story time).

The prospect of providing virtual services for teens required unique consideration by libraries—if it was considered at all. While library systems might treat in-person teen activities as an extension of children/tween services, the use of virtual platforms serves to expose vital differences between the two. Libraries may have approached the use of online platforms for teen activities with the same lack of clarity with which they approach planning in-person teen activities. Their efforts may also have achieved the same discouraging results. Offering in-person teen activities may have already been a challenging proposition for public libraries in the best of times. Planning may occur in library landscapes where the notion of teen activities is not well conceptualized or defined or where they may be considered expendable when compared with other library services, such as children's services. Libraries make assumptions about teen interests; teen needs; and most essentially, what age range constitutes this user group. Providing teen activities may be so confounding to some libraries that these services are simply not offered or they are offered to "aspirational teens," those ages 9 through 12. Additionally, consider that teen activities often lack a traditional format beyond the sometimes impractical "teen advisory boards" and may not be considered an "expected" core service.

Contrast this with children's keystone service—the story time. In most public libraries, a story time that took place in 2010 did not look vastly different from a story time that took place in 1910. The trappings and techniques may be different, but in both, the essence is the same: An adult faces a group of children and reads a story from a book. Children sit facing the librarian and listen to the reading. In both, the librarian selects the books, crafts, songs, or other activities. In both, the librarian is framed as creator/presenter and the user as receiver/audience. The type of planning that takes place to produce a children's story time aligns with the capacities of the user group.

Translating a story time to the virtual space of a platform, such as YouTube, does not essentially change the placement of the user. Whether "live" or recorded, the roles remain essentially the same: The librarian is creator/presenter, and the child is receiver/audience. Indeed, recordings of story time work via one-way communication because while interaction with children is desirable, it is not necessary for a successful outcome.

When the shutdown precipitated the shift to virtual, imagine the likelihood of teens, with their myriad of digital content/social network choices and low parental mediation, voluntarily choosing to watch a recording of a librarian presenting a teen activity. As with all public library services, teens are not required to participate/attend (as in school), nor are the services delivered (by parents, as in children's story time) to a public library's teen activity whether in person or online.

SITUATING THE TEEN USER IN PERSON AND ONLINE

Librarians have problematic assumptions about teen activities and these are learned. Assumptions can manifest early and remain present throughout the life cycle of a librarian's career—from education to practice. This likely occurs because there is no established, standard "recipe" for teen activities (as there is for a children's story time) beyond the often obligatory but poorly conceptualized teen advisory board. Initially, library and information science (LIS) education taught mimicry of children's services activity planning process as an approach to teen services. Courses requiring LIS students to "plan programs" for teens by selecting adult-generated "hot ideas," presumed of interest to teens, set a librarian up for failure in the real-world library setting. Once working with teens, librarians framing themselves as presenters and their interests/agendas as topics for teen activities will likely not provide valuable services. Teens will vote with their feet.

Ideally, teen activities should be conceived, developed, and implemented by teens for themselves and their peers with minimal adult (librarian) mediation. Teen users should be situated as creators of activities rather than as audience/participants at librarian-created programs. To "situate a user" of a library service means to place users within a specific context or environment, considering user expectations as well as library service goals. Libraries (should) situate users of activities by considering users' capacities and preferences and (should) devise planning structures that support these accordingly.

The core responsibility of librarians in teen activity planning is not planning at all—but facilitation. Librarians must understand that their role is to step out of the way and foster/facilitate the activity planning undertaken by teens.

Translating a teen activity to the virtual space on a platform, such as Discord, can cultivate and maintain a high level of teen participation, decision-making, and ownership. The goal is for staff to become surplus on the server and though we know teens value the relationship building that occurs with library staff, recede or, at the very most, help facilitate a club until teens take control. Discord use situates the teen user in the same way successful in-person teen activities do—with teens developing and implementing activities with minimal adult (librarian) mediation.

DISCORD OVERCOMES BARRIERS OF IN-PERSON TEEN ACTIVITIES

Using Discord not only overcame the challenge of the shutdown but also provided an opportunity to examine how the use of an online platform dissolves some operational barriers inherent in in-person teen activities. While the primary barrier to successful in-person teen activities is a lack of dedicated teen services staff, innate operational barriers impede success to even the most well-rendered services. For example, the location of the library itself may be a constraint. Teens may rely on parents or public transportation to get to the library location and may not be able to depend on these to arrive on the date/time of in-person teen activities. Additionally, the schedule of teen activities can be a barrier. If teen activities take place erratically, or even if they are consistently scheduled, the date/time of the activity may not conform to the teens' schedule.

In libraries, physical space to conduct in-person teen activities may also be limited or may constrain the types of activities that may take place (i.e., the perceived problem of conducting video gaming, music exploration, or painting on the general service floor). Teen services may also face the barrier of competition for use of meeting room space to conduct activities if a teen space is nonexistent. Virtual activities diminish these in-person barriers. On a Discord server, for example, hundreds of channels (clubs) reflecting teen interests may be created, and interactions can take place 24/7. Activities and interactions take place where teens "are" via their personal devices. Activities and interactions take place outside the restraints of scheduling limitations, meeting room usage, and staff availability. The online clubs may take place with no/low adult mediation beyond the creation of the requested channels.

Additionally, teens gathering in a physical library space are brought together by proximity to the library's location. This provides exposure to a variety of interests from a variety of other teens who are forging exploration of new subjects and ideas. The same can be said of an online venue, which has the additional benefit of teens being able to easily gather in channels based on specific interests.

BUILDING A FOUNDATION FOR VIRTUAL TEEN SERVICES

The use of Discord revealed the benefit of being where teens "are" in the online space and using a familiar, popular online venue to foster connections with teens and the library. Libraries that attempted to use Discord during the COVID shutdown or that are currently seeking to use Discord for teen activities may find limited success if they apply outmoded teen activity planning habits to this novel venue. They may plan, post, and host a teen book club on a Discord server with similarly weak degrees of success as they find in the in-person setting. A Discord server must be built with teens. The goal of a Discord server is to ultimately have it run by teen users—just as genuinely successful in-person programming must be devised and implemented by teens for themselves and their peers. In both, the foundation is the same, and libraries experiencing limited success with Discord efforts would benefit from examining their approach to in-person teen activities. The approach must be the same even if the venues are different.

However, even as the activity planning approach for in-person and online activities should be the same, there are some unique considerations for libraries wishing to undertake the use of an online venue like Discord for teen activities or to evaluate the application of an existing Discord server for teens.

24/7 AND TRUSTING TEENS

Limiting Discord use only to "programming" times or "opening" Discord only during scheduled days/times preserves barriers found in in-person teen activities. Ideally, a teen Discord server should be available outside of library business hours. Yes, this suggests there will be times when staff members are not present. Teens must be trusted to maintain and moderate their space. It's vital to deploy teen volunteers and moderators on a teen Discord server. This is not only the backbone of teen ownership/participation, but teen moderators are vital to cultivating a dynamic, large, responsive server. Lack of trust in teens to take on the role as moderators in their space or the inability to use their space 24/7 will impede the success of activities and interactions. It is essential that teens "own" and run their server in the same way they should in-person activities.

AVOIDING PRESCRIBED EXPERIENCES

Teen librarians may envision Discord as a platform for devising prescribed experiences for teens (i.e., clever or educational "program ideas") rather than guiding teens toward creation, autonomy, and ownership—just as librarians might do in face-to-face activities. Keeping channels broad and offering a place for teens to suggest specific channels help to fine-tune a server to the specific interests of its unique teen users.

LOW ADULT (LIBRARIAN) MEDIATION

Disruptive adult mediation must be limited. Library staff will be present on the Discord server, but their interactions with teens must be restrained and should not constitute adult mediation. Discord servers where librarians clumsily inject themselves or monopolize conversation risks shutting down teen discussion and result in awkwardness among teen users. If a conversation between teens is happening, the last contribution needed is the opinion of an adult (librarian). Otherwise, the risk of librarians talking to each other to "start a conversation" could be realized, rather than librarians facilitating teen expression and ownership.

STAFF TIME COMMITMENT

A successful teen Discord server requires adequate library staff, and librarians may simply not have adequate time to dedicate to the rigors of a virtual teen

Jennifer Velásquez

branch. Running a Discord server for teens in a library setting is a "handcrafted" proposition, akin to running a branch location. It requires a great deal of maintenance and "back-of-house" work, which can only be accomplished by dedicated staff with enough time. Libraries must provide adequate staff/time to accomplish the goal of successful and meaningful Discord use.

The issues discussed here, as considerations for Discord use, are certainly not exhaustive. For a full case study of the development of the @210teenlibrary Discord server, see Prukop and Loazia (2022).

CONCLUSION

Early in the COVID shutdown, a teen messaged staff on the @210teenlibrary server asking, "We are going to keep doing this, right?"—meaning, will the library continue providing the Discord server once branches reopen for in-person teen activities? This question came way before the server had matured into the robust venue it is today, but it offered the first sign that use of the online platform had resonance beyond the shutdown.

Use of the Discord platform resolved the immediate challenge of providing service and activities for teens while maintaining a high degree of teen agency/autonomy/ownership over their library experience. Beyond the initial resolution, the use of the server offered the opportunity to decrease challenges inherent in in-person teen activities. After the shutdown, its use helps illustrate the contrast between children/tween activities and teen activities and reveals pervasive flaws/opportunities in the planning of all teen activities.

Because the physical library has constraints, digital platforms such as Discord can complement in-person activities, offering opportunities for interaction beyond the library's physical limitations. The @210teenlibrary Discord server has become an expected service: a new venue for the library to be open in different ways.

DISCUSSION QUESTIONS

- Under what other circumstances might a library explore a virtual service response?
- What resources or strategies might be brought to bear to address some of the "pitfalls" Velasquez identifies?

REFERENCE

Prukop, S., & Loazia, M. (2022). Using Discord to create a harmonious space for teens. *Computers in Libraries*, *42*(6), 8–12.

3

Outreach, Community, and Connections for Readers and Teachers Using Social Media

Jennifer Burek Pierce and Jackie Biger

Whether librarians work in public or school libraries, librarians recommend books to young people and teachers. Librarians must learn the features of books that can respond to young readers' interests and needs and to the instructional goals of teachers in their school. Following our discussion of these principles, we recommend an assignment that supports librarians' ability to communicate about books, highlighting the importance of including picture books as beneficial for all young people.

This project operates at the intersections of two areas of our profession, youth services and school librarianship, and our preface to the assignment itself reflects the terminology and the priorities of these areas. It focuses attention on the genre or format known as the picture book, represented by some experts as *picturebook*. As discussed in Hodges and Matthews (2017), picture books have value for all readers and learners, regardless of age. The project supports librarians' development of core skills in readers' advisory, reviewing, and public communication. It rests on the idea that readers have choices, allowing library and information science (LIS) students to make their own choices about the picture books they rely on as part of their coursework. The assignment and the skills that must be taught to support it, then, are multifaceted and complex, resting on rationales for using picture books with older readers.

The assignment grows our students' skills in reading picture books and in communicating with multiple potential audiences that they will encounter in their professional lives. It supports the idea that picture books, rather than being part of a teen's reading past, should continue to feature in the texts they encounter as they age. Librarians who work with young adults in either school or public libraries can use picture books as mentor texts, which explain or anchor a concept for readers and can also be reread to reveal new ideas or layers of meaning and the craft of writing with repetition. The study by Premont et al. (2017) concludes that the integration of picture books in classrooms helped adolescents of all skill levels improve in writing conventions. In an article on mentor texts, Laminack (2017) explores the idea of mentorship and the use of familiar and accessible books as a source of comfort and resource. Beyond the concept of the mentor text, there are multiple reasons for sharing picture books with teens. We know that the work librarians do with picture books shapes the culture and the experience of teen readers. Spending time in a shared moment of reading builds community. Further, we know that as young people age, they are read to less and less; teachers and librarians, though, testify to the enjoyment and relationships that emerge when they read to teens. In schools, picture books can support us in defining a concept and providing background knowledge that creates the necessary scaffolding into a lesson. Additionally, a reality of some teens' lives is that they are caregivers for younger children, whether their own infants or children in their family, and modeling the importance of reading together can affect reading lives generationally.

Sharing picture books with teens is important. As we work with new librarians in our classes, helping them understand how picture books can serve the needs of adolescents, as well as younger readers, offers them rewarding strategies for engaging with books in both school and public library settings. The assignment that explains to our students how to document their picture book reading and to practice public communication as a librarian follows. Preceding the first online posts for this assignment, we recommend a workshop that allows students to practice and reflect on a draft post, receiving faculty feedback before sharing their content more widely.

INSTAGRAM YOUR READINGS: RECURRING ASSIGNMENT

You will select some of your own required course readings of picture books, and you will document and share those readings using Instagram. We will use both conventions of the platform and those specific to our course to fulfill the requirements for this ongoing project, as outlined on this assignment sheet. This activity prepares you to discuss media professionally and to use social media for library and reading advocacy.

THE BASICS

As designated on the syllabus, each week you will review four books that relate to the topic on which we focused during that class session. At least one of these books must be a picture book suited to the age cohort we are studying. Select and read your books by the next class meeting, but you may complete your online posts following the class discussion of these titles.

CREATE AN INSTAGRAM ACCOUNT

If you already have an Instagram account, you may use it; however, you should consider whether it might be beneficial to create an account specifically for this project:

- Do you post on behalf of a school, library, or other employer? If you do so from an extant account, it may be best to create a new account to avoid potential problems with policy and identity.
- Do you post with content that might be described by the contemporary phrase Not Safe for Work (NSFW) or by the more subtle word *mature*? Both to avoid confusing your own brand and the content associated with this university course, it might be best to have a separate account for this project.

Consider the identity you wish to establish when you create and select a name for your account. It's fine to have an account that is anonymous:

- You can use words that are not part of your name, school, or location.
- You can use an image or avatar for your account that is not a picture of you.
- At the same time, though, avoid images that might be seen as copyright infringement or misleading, like a name that too closely plays on an established public figure or celebrity.

FOR EACH WEEK'S SELF-SELECTED READING ASSIGNMENT

Plan and edit the content for your selections. Consider whether a single post, with all images and reviews, is the best way to present the content or whether you will make four separate posts.

If creating a single post for all your reviews, plan on submitting one image along with the review for each of the books selected. The reviews must also be shared via what Instagram calls the *Caption* space. The review for each book should be approximately 75 to 100 words, as is the norm for reviews in *Library Journal* and *School Library Journal*. One simple reality of online communication is that unless you have an established audience, most readers will not read lengthy communications. We will examine and practice this technique in a workshop before your first post.

If you are creating a post for each of your selections and accompanying reviews, then you might use one to four photos, while still maintaining the brevity of the review and the other required elements.

Following are the required elements of your post:

- Title, author, and year of publication
- Expected age range of readers
- Topic or subject of the book
- Required hashtags designating the course, program, and/or university

The following elements may be useful to your review commentary:

- Genre and/or medium
- Tone or approach to the subject
- Purpose or potential use of the book
- Illustration technique and effect
- Takeaways, like what is depicted or what the book seems to do (A lesson about friendship? Conquering fears? Insights into a little-known subject? A great book on a subject that draws lots of interest? And so on)
- Connections to Common Core standards to highlight support of school curriculum (particularly important if you are a school librarian)
- Relevant hashtags, either from the table below or from your own research or knowledge
- A simple summary does not meet the requirements for this assignment

Avoid @'ing authors and illustrators unless these people have a declared, current, or published interest in hearing from people this way. Because popular authors may have so many people tagging them, use hashtags with the creator's name, book title, or series instead. Think of the use of the hashtag over the @ as online etiquette, much the way we do not post in all caps if we're not shouting.

Our purpose is to participate in an online conversation about the picture books we would want in our collections and as part of our programming. These posts are not created for the purpose of calling out authors or illustrators, becoming part of cancel culture, and so on. If you read a book that you find objectionable, we can discuss it in class, but you should plan to select an alternative for your public post.

Hashtags are an important part of this assignment. Much like MARC records denote classification, subject headings, and a way to filter collection items based on search terms, hashtags can serve this function as well. We recommend having required hashtags that will allow you to search and interact with your peers but also for you to practice classification, subject, interest, and Common Core alignment with the use of hashtags alongside book commentaries. The hashtags should be consistent and usable for their audience of readers. Because some of you are practicing school librarians, we encourage you to build an audience using relevant hashtags specific to your school district as well. Some hashtags include #bookskidslove, #childrensbookstagram, #diversebooksforkids, #picturebooks, #mentortext, #schoollibrarian, and #commoncore (include subject area).

CONCLUSION

Our students have been excited about connecting with other professionals, authors, and illustrators as the result of their social media work. They also gain communication skills that they share with potential employers, conceptualizing how online communications contribute to the library brand and its outreach voice. Additionally, they model for their own students the social thread of sharing books, an increasing activity across platforms. While this assignment was developed for Instagram, it can be adapted and applied to other platforms, depending on the needs of your community. This kind of advocacy can also be used in other professional communication contexts, like the sharing and reflection among staff members or with teachers. Using social media for communicating about books is a burgeoning area of activity that lacks robust professional or research documentation, although there is an emergent literature on teens and BookTok (see, for example, research by Jeresa & Boffone, 2021; Martens et al., 2022; and Meggs, 2021). In addition to using this assignment, teachers and librarians could publish the outcomes of their work in this area, whether focused on young people's class-based or avocational reading.

DISCUSSION QUESTIONS

- What percentage of a young adult librarian's collection development time should be devoted to picture books?
- What challenges might a young adult librarian face in collecting picture books for teens?

REFERENCES

Hodges, T. S., & Matthews, S. D. (2017). Picture books aren't just for kids! Modeling text structures through nonfiction mentor books. *Voices from the Middle, 24*(4), 74.

Jerasa, S., & Boffone, T. (2021). Booktok 101: TikTok, digital literacies, and out of school reading practices. *Journal of Adolescent and Adult Literacy, 65*(3), 219–26.

Laminack, L. (2017). Mentors and mentor texts: What, why, and how? *The Reading Teacher, 70*(6), 753–55.

Martens, M., Balling, G., & Higgason, K. (2022). #BookTokMadeMeReadIt: Young adult reading communities across an international, sociotechnical landscape. *Information and Learning Sciences, 123*(11/12), 705–22.

Meggs, M. (2021). How can Booktok inform readers' advisory services for young people? *Library & Information Science Research, 43*(2). https://doi.org/10.1016/j.lisr.2021.101091.

Premont, D. W., Young, T. A., Wilcox, B., Dean, D., & Morrison, T. G. (2017). Picture books as mentor texts for 10th grade struggling writers. *Literacy Research and Instruction, 56*(4), 290–310.

4

The Challenges of Defining Outreach Services to Underserved Teens

Jess Snow

Discussing outreach is difficult in that there is no definition that has been adopted by all libraries, library systems, and/or mentioned in job descriptions. The American Library Association (ALA) Office for Diversity, Literacy, and Outreach Services defines *outreach* as "providing library services and programs outside the walls of the library to underserved and underrepresented populations; populations such as new and non-readers, LGBTQIA people, people of color, poor and homeless people, and people who are incarcerated" (para. 3-4). Several libraries do utilize this definition, and it can be seen in their strategic plans, on their websites, and in their work with underserved teens.

To understand what outreach services mean, the history is helpful in piecing together a definition that reveals the beginnings of the practice. In doing so, two issues begin to emerge:

1. There is no distinction drawn between outreach services to children and outreach services to teens, these two service populations are often commingled as either "young people" or "children," thereby making it difficult to identify instances where outreach services were provided specifically to teens.
2. There is no universally accepted definition for outreach services.

Kathleen Weibel's thesis, *The Evolution of Library Outreach 1960-75, and its Effect on Reader Services*, published in 1982 states that

The history is murky due to several factors. One factor is that we do not see the use of the word *outreach* until around the 1960s. This has more to do with the civil rights movement, the extensive media coverage of the violence and conflicts that erupted in cities across the country, and America's awakening to the harsh reality of poverty and what was billed as an all-out attack on the problems of the poor. Another factor, as mentioned above, is that there is no distinction between children and teens as service populations; when outreach *was* talked about, it was in regard to "young people." The history of outreach focuses, more generally, on all ages with youth peppered in here and there.

When we think of the history of outreach services, we begin in 1901, when the librarian Mary Lemist Titcomb of the Washington County Free Library in Hagerstown, Maryland, began a mobile library using a horse-drawn wagon. She set up book-deposit stations in remote rural areas so that patrons could have access to books. After four years, there were 66 such stations. Titcomb undertook these new and innovative services because she knew of patrons who were unable to get to the library and its resources. Her focus on reaching underserved populations and her strategic approach attracted the attention of the Washington County Free Library Board of Trustees. They provided funding for an additional wagon to begin providing mobile services in their community. As Mary Titcomb said at the ALA Annual Conference in 1909, "The book goes to the man. We do not wait for the man to come to the book" (p. 151). This is the focus of outreach, to bring the services and the books outside of the library to the people. It is all about access.

It was not until the 1920s that ALA involved itself in the issue of providing services to populations that were unable to access library services. This was the beginning of a focus on mobile or outreach services along with the creation of ALA's Committee on Library Extension in 1925. The committee looked at ways to extend library services to unserved areas in the United States. Their focus was on rural libraries, particularly those in the South.

Beginning in the 1930s, we see the Pack Horse Library Project, a Works Progress Administration (WPA) effort that ran from 1935 to 1943, which provided mobile library services to the remote coves and mountainsides of Kentucky and nearby Appalachia. Sometimes, these "packhorse librarians" relied on a centralized contact to help with the distribution of materials. They provided "people" access to library resources, but the history does not specify any demographic attributes other than "remote peoples." It really isn't until the 1960s that we begin to see a differentiation by age being used in relation to the service population. For example, the "Library in Action" was a late 1960s book-mobile program in the Bronx, New York, which was run by an interracial staff who brought books to teenagers of color in underserved neighborhoods. I was unable to find out more about this bookmobile program, but the fact that it was run by an interracial staff shows they were thinking about *who* they were serving and about *representation* in this racially diverse community. These librarians wanted to serve teens, and they were purposefully going to areas where library services were not saturated. In 1968, Minudri and Coates, two young adult librarians in Santa Clara County, California, set up satellite collections in teen centers and provided mobile library services to those that did not have library cards. There was a very deliberate and purposeful focus on serving the underserved in urban public libraries during the 1960s. As Craver (1988) observes,

> [i]n several cities, libraries were established in nontraditional settings to help lower the barriers erected by formidable library architecture and bureaucratic procedures. While most of these libraries/centers were established for the entire community, each contained a young adult service component. In several instances, libraries/centers were designed solely for young adults. (p. 32)

In the twenty-first century, some public libraries began to formally define outreach and explicitly articulate the meaning and scope of this service. Their work with teens captures and supports ALA's definition. For example, the Charlotte Mecklenburg Public Library provides a separate page within the library's website that speaks directly to what outreach services mean, what those services provide, and whom they are aiming to reach with these services. Similarly, the Brooklyn Public Library offers an excellent definition of outreach on a separate web page. The New York Public Library, along with each of its branches, not only offers outreach services tailored to teens but also explicitly outlines the scope of these services and provides a clear definition of outreach. While there are other examples, these libraries excel at articulating who they serve and what these services entail and describing the staff members responsible for serving these populations. Who are these populations?

- Teens who are or were incarcerated. On any given night in the United States, more than 15,000 teens are incarcerated (Annie E. Casey Foundation, 2021). This number is as of 2017.
- Youth in foster care. According to the most recent federal data, there are currently more than 400,000 youth in foster care in the United States. They range in age from infants to 21 years old (in some states) (Annie E. Casey Foundation, 2021).
- Youth who are immigrants. Approximately 17.8 million US children under age 18 lived with at least one immigrant parent in 2019. They accounted for 26 percent of the 68.9 million children (about twice the population of

California) under age 18 in the United States, up from 19 percent in 2000 and 13 percent in 1990 (Ward & Batalova, 2023).

- Refugee youth. To obtain refugee status, a person who has fled their home needs to demonstrate a well-founded fear of persecution based on race, religion, nationality, political opinion, or membership in a particular social group. In fiscal year 2020, the United States resettled fewer than 12,000 refugees. This is quite different from the 70,000 to 80,000 refugees resettled annually just a few years earlier and the 207,000 welcomed in 1980, the year the formal US resettlement program began (Monin et al., 2021).
- Unhoused youth. In an average 12-month period, 1 in 30 young people become unhoused, which is about 700,000 youth per year (Morton et al., 2017).
- Youth attending alternative schools. Alternative schools were established in the 1970s to meet the needs of children and adolescents who are not able to learn in traditional school environments. This might be due to learning disabilities, certain medical conditions, and psychological and behavioral issues. In general, alternative schools have more comprehensive educational and developmental objectives than conventional schools. There are about 800,000 teens enrolled in alternative schools (Kho & Rabovsky, 2022).
- Youth in drug and alcohol recovery. There are schools in the United States that are operated through the city school system, and there are alternative schools that can address some of the issues that these teens may be facing.
- LGBT youth. Of teens aged 13 to 17, 1.9 million identify as LGBT (Conron, 2020).
- Young parents.

These are some examples of the teen populations needing outreach services with which you could connect. How do you go about finding and connecting with them?

You might want to start by looking at the census to get a sense of the demographic makeup of a specific group or community. Census data includes the percentage of people living in poverty and the percentage of people who have or do not have computers and/or internet connectivity as well as data on racial demographics, age distribution, and other relevant factors. This can give you a sense of who is in your user community. You can also check to see if there are social service agencies, such as the Department of Children and Families. These agencies work in partnership with families and communities to keep children in foster care safe from abuse and neglect. Is there a juvenile detention facility? Like the Department of Children and Families, this state agency serves youth who are incarcerated. By searching your state website, you can learn about this agency, what they do, and where they are located.

From the census, you can gain insight into the immigrant and refugee populations in your city. Using this information, you can conduct a straightforward search like "refugee organizations near me." Search results will provide an overview of some of these organizations in your community, their missions, and the populations they serve. In many cities, you will find organizations that work with various demographics, such as those dedicated to assisting unhoused populations. For instance, you might come across a homeless shelter coalition. Their primary mission is to proactively plan, conduct policy analyses, develop programs, and advocate for measures aimed at preventing and alleviating homelessness and hunger. They achieve this through close collaboration with city, state, federal, and community partner agencies. They work directly with the city's homeless and homeless families.

Think about the city you are in and get a sense of the agencies that may work with some of these populations. You can also look at the state and federal websites to familiarize yourself with some of the agencies and policies that might be useful. For example, the McKinney-Vento Act of 1987 was enacted to eliminate barriers for parents or caregivers experiencing homelessness. This federal law allows for the immediate enrollment of homeless youth in school, even if they lack the necessary documents or have missed application or enrollment deadlines. It ensures that support is available for children and teens experiencing homelessness, which includes those who are homeless due to loss of housing; are sharing the home of others; staying in motels, trailer parks, or campgrounds; staying in shelters or transitional housing; or sleeping in cars, parks, abandoned buildings, substandard housing, and similar settings.

Every local education agency must designate a liaison for unhoused students who is able to carry out the duties described in the law. This means that in every state, city, and town, there are liaisons who work directly with youth experiencing homelessness. Identifying these liaisons is typically straightforward because they are often affiliated with the local school system in a city or town. Additionally, other agencies may collaborate in supporting youth who are homeless. These liaisons serve as valuable resources and make excellent partners for outreach efforts.

What about young parents? This would mean working with teens and with children. There are alternative schools that work with teen parents as well as organizations that provide services directly to both the parents and the children. A straightforward query such as "young parent organizations near me" can yield useful results if there are relevant organizations in your city. This is a broad enough search to provide relevant information. Sometimes, hospitals extend their services to this population. You might also discover schools that cater to this demographic. Additionally, you may come across umbrella organizations, such as the Annie E. Casey Foundation, which are national entities providing a wide range of services to various populations. These organizations often consist of related, industry-specific institutions collaborating formally to coordinate activities or pool resources. What are some twenty-first-century challenges in providing outreach to underserved teens?

STAFFING

The belief that one must be tied to a desk or that teens will simply come to the library is based on an outdated staffing model. The twenty-first-century service model should focus on going where the teens are. However, staffing models currently employed in most public libraries are outmoded in that there is a focus on serving teens *in the library*, which disregards outreach. This means there are often issues with waiting for teens to visit the library and consistently staffing the desk. But this can be remedied! Outreach also involves advocating for the services your user group needs. Creating and presenting an outreach services plan to your director or supervisor, which includes a consistent day and time when these services will be conducted, is a great way to start. If your supervisor is aware that you will be conducting outreach every first Friday from 9:00 to 11:00 a.m., it can be scheduled and noted on the calendar. If this time aligns with staff availability, you are likely to receive more support from your supervisor.

In the Public Library Association (PLA) 2021 Public Library Staff and Diversity Survey, a total of 773 city, suburban, and rural libraries participated in the survey (PLA, 2021). The survey included two open-ended questions that inquired about the types of roles these libraries had hired staff for in the past 12 months and the types of roles they would like to create if funding were available.

Regarding the first question, 41 percent of the libraries (out of 234 responses) reported hiring staff in core service areas and support services. These areas encompass access, collections, reference, technical services, and other roles related to support staff and paraprofessionals. Notably, there is a growing trend in staffing focused on community engagement, outreach, and public-facing work, which has become increasingly important due to the changes and challenges posed by the pandemic. Specifically, 41.9 percent of respondents reported hiring new staff in these areas. When considering the roles libraries would like to create with additional funding, a similar pattern emerges. Forty percent of libraries (out of 467 responses) expressed interest in creating roles within core service areas, with an additional 4.7 percent specifying managerial or leadership roles. However, a significant 67 percent of libraries indicated their desire to establish new positions in community engagement, outreach, and public programs.

Furthermore, the survey inquired about whether libraries had formal, written goals for equity, diversity, and inclusion. Among those libraries that responded affirmatively, the focus of these goals varied. Notably, 79 percent of city libraries reported having goals that specifically target outreach, while the figures for suburban and rural libraries were 79.6 and 65.4 percent, respectively, in terms of having direct outreach-related goals.

THE DEFINITION OF "OUTREACH" IN JOB DESCRIPTIONS

Even in job descriptions for positions like "Teen Outreach Librarians," the definition of what outreach entails is frequently missing. This lack of clarity places the responsibility on the librarian and more importantly, on the library itself to establish and articulate a precise understanding of outreach services. Without a clear definition, librarians may not fully comprehend their roles or continue to provide these critical services effectively.

Some library systems do provide explicit definitions of outreach on dedicated "outreach" web pages, which also specify the target audience. However, when it comes to job descriptions for positions such as teen or young adult librarians with an outreach focus, they often fall short in outlining expectations or defining the intended beneficiaries of the services. In such cases, it becomes the responsibility of the librarian to proactively investigate the library's existing outreach partners and examine the strategic plan to determine if "outreach" is identified as a focal area of emphasis.

THE LACK OF FOCUS ON TEEN SERVICES IN MOST PUBLIC LIBRARIES

This is not a new issue. The public library has a long history of unsatisfactory services to teens. We can go back to the beginnings of outreach to see the difficulty in even identifying teen populations because they were often commingled with children—the more established user group. Children's services were developed before teen services because teens (adolescents) were not identified as a separate and specific stage of human development until 1904 (by G. Stanley Hall). The Association for Library Service to Children (ALSC) was established in 1900; in contrast, the Young Adult Services Division (now the Young Adult Library Services Association, or YALSA) wasn't founded until 1957. This division was specifically established to address the unique needs and interests of teenagers in library settings. The creation of YALSA marked the formal recognition of young adult library services within the field. Unfortunately, it did not signify the beginning of satisfactory teen services.

As stated in *The Value of Continuous Teen Services* (YALSA, 2018), school and public libraries frequently

- tolerate negative staff attitudes toward teens;
- plan programs without first seeking teen input, which often leads to low attendance;

- Struggle to create formal and informal learning experiences for teens that amplify youth voice, incorporate community engagement, and focus on high-quality outcomes; and
- overlook the positive impact year-round services have on teens' learning, engagement, and life outcomes as well as on the library's perceived value by community members.

Additionally, many public libraries tend to

- focus most of their resources, including staff time, for teen services in the summer months (it is during the school year when many teens need library help) and
- schedule programs to take place in the library, thus limiting participation to those teens who have access to reliable transportation

WORKABLE SOLUTIONS

How can you advocate for your library to provide outreach services to under-served teens?

Start at the beginning. Is your library providing any outreach to teens? Has it ever and if so, to whom?

What does your strategic plan say? Does it look at focusing services outside of the library to underserved populations? Are there buzzwords like *outreach, community engagement, underserved,* or *connecting with the community*? Take a good look at that strategic plan, find those words and ideas, and connect your ideas of outreach to underserved teens to that of the focus of the library.

What does your job description say? Is outreach in your job description? If so, have a conversation with administration and/or your supervisor and get a sense of what they see as outreach and whom you could connect with and how? What is the expectation of your library and what is your expectation?

What are the demographics in your city, town, suburb? Are there un-derserved teen populations? Find them, cite them, and share them with your administration. Plan to connect with those populations.

What are the priorities of the city/town/suburb you are in? Tie this out-reach work to priorities of your city/town/suburb and the focus of the mayor. Because public libraries are city/town agencies, it is important to be aware of the initiatives of your town. Are you able to tie that work into the initiatives of your city/town/suburb?

Make a recommendation of services to underserved teens complete with a plan, time commitment, goals, and outcomes, and share that with adminis-tration and/or your supervisor.

CONCLUSION

In conclusion, many libraries and librarians are providing outreach services. Often it can look uneven and detached from the library's strategic plan. But it can also be consistent, thorough, and purposeful. We may have to advocate in our own libraries to be able to provide outreach to underserved teens. We may be in a library with a well-defined outreach services model and/or an outreach services department. Nevertheless, it will always be important to look outside the library—to know the community in which we serve, to gain a sense of the underserved teen population in our community, and most importantly, to determine whom we are not serving in our libraries.

DISCUSSION QUESTIONS

- What measures might young adult librarians establish to demonstrate outreach success?
- How might young adults themselves be recruited to assist with outreach activities?
- What sources of local information might a young adult librarian search to discover nonschool targets/audiences for outreach activities?

REFERENCES

Annie E. Casey Foundation. (2021). *Juvenile detention explained.* https://www.aecf.org/blog/what-is-juvenile-detention.

Conron, K. J. (2020). *LGBT youth population in the United States.* UCLA School of Law Williams Institute. https://williamsinstitute.law.ucla.edu/wp-content/uploads/LGBT-Youth-US-Pop-Sep-2020.pdf.

Craver, K. W. (1988). Social trends in American young adult library service, 1960-1969. *Libraries & Culture, 23*(1), 18–38.

Kho, A., & Rabovsky, S. (2022). *The students alternative schools serve.* Urban Institute. https://www.urban.org/research/publication/students-alternative-schools-serve#:~:text=Key%20Data,school%20students%20attend%20urban%20schools.

Monin, K., Batalova, J., & Lai, T. (2021). *Refugees and asylees in the United States.* Migration Policy Institute. https://www.migrationpolicy.org/article/refugees-and-asylees-united-states-2021.

Morton, M. H., Dworsky, A., & Samuels, G. M. (2017). *Missed opportunities: Youth homelessness in America: National estimates.* Chapin Hall at the University of Chicago. https://voicesofyouthcount.org/brief/national-estimates-of-youth-homelessness/.

Public Library Association (PLA). (2021). *Public library staff and diversity report results from the 2021 PLA annual survey.* https://www.ala.org/pla/sites/ala.org.pla/files/content/data/PLA_Staff_Survey_Report_2022.pdf.

Titcomb, M. (1909). *Papers and Proceedings of the Thirty-First Annual Meeting of the American Library Association, Chicago.* Record Series 5/1/2, American Library Association Archives, University of Illinois at Urbana-Champaign.

Ward, N., & Batalova, J. (2023). *Frequently requested statistics on immigrants and immigration in the United States.* Migration Policy Institute. https://www.migration policy.org/article/frequently-requested-statistics-immigrants-and-immigration -united-states#:~:text=Approximately%2017.8%20million%20U.S.%20children ,and%2013%20percent%20in%201990.

Weibel, K. (1982). *The evolution of library outreach 1960-75 and its effect on reader services.* University of Illinois Graduate School of Library and Information Science. https:// core.ac.uk/download/pdf/4813998.pdf.

Young Adult Library Services Association (YALSA). (2018). *The value of continuous teen services: A YALSA position paper.* https://www.ala.org/yalsa/value-continuous -teen-services-yalsa-position-paper.

5

Unleashing the Power of Hip Hop

CATALYST FOR EQUITABLE LIBRARY SERVICES FOR YOUNG ADULTS

Kafi D. Kumasi

Like hip hop, a youth librarian's work is oriented toward empowering youth through creative forms of engagement that reflect their voice, interests, and talents. And like hip hop, a youth librarian's scope of work is ever changing to keep up with new media forms of expression that keep youth audiences hyped and engaged. Hip hop represents the voice of youth from marginalized communities and has emerged as a potent force of expression, activism, and identity formation. Yet one of the core challenges youth librarianship faces is that it implicitly privileges whiteness at the expense of knowing and being indigenous to people of color, which embrace orality, rhythm, and movement over finite, linear ways of knowing that have been associated with whiteness. As libraries strive to provide equitable services for young adults, harnessing the power of hip hop can revolutionize the way we engage and connect with this demographic. By embracing hip hop culture, libraries can dismantle barriers, amplify diverse voices, and foster a truly inclusive and transformative space for young adults.

THE CULTURAL SIGNIFICANCE OF HIP HOP ON YOUTH

Originating from the Bronx in the 1970s, hip hop quickly transcended its musical origins to become a powerful artistic and sociopolitical movement. Hip hop serves as a vital platform for marginalized voices, empowering communities and offering a creative outlet for young adults to express their experiences, challenges, and aspirations. Through its elements of music, dance, visual art, fashion, storytelling, and street entrepreneurialism, hip hop provides a rich tapestry of cultural expression that resonates deeply with young adults from diverse backgrounds. Prior to 2020, hip hop had become the dominant genre in terms of overall music consumption in the United States. According to the Nielsen 2019 Year-End Report, hip hop surpassed rock as the most consumed genre, accounting for 28.2 percent of total music consumption. By offering a space for artistic expression, self-discovery, and community building, hip hop can provide youth with a means of cultural expression, personal growth, and social activism.

PROMOTING EQUITY AND SOCIAL JUSTICE

Hip hop, at its core, is deeply rooted in social justice and activism. Hip hop emerged as a platform for marginalized communities, particularly African Americans and Latinos, to express their experiences and perspectives. It provides a voice for people living in disenfranchised neighborhoods, addressing issues such as police brutality, systemic racism, economic disparities, and social injustice. Hip hop has a long history of political activism with artists like Public Enemy, Dead Prez, and NWA, among many others, who have used their music as a form of protest against racial injustice, government policies, and societal inequities. Libraries can amplify this aspect by engaging young adults in critical conversations around social issues through hip hop–themed book clubs, discussions, and workshops. By exploring the sociopolitical themes embedded within hip hop, young adults are encouraged to challenge systemic inequalities and envision a more equitable world.

BREAKING BARRIERS THROUGH HIP HOP

Libraries, as guardians of knowledge, have the responsibility to create spaces that are accessible and relevant to all young adults. Incorporating hip hop into library services breaks down barriers by meeting young adults where they are culturally and engaging them in a way that resonates. Here are key ways hip hop can transform library services:

1. Hip hop collections: Libraries can curate collections that reflect the breadth and depth of hip hop culture, encompassing music albums, biographies, poetry, graphic novels, and literature that celebrate the voices and experiences of hip hop artists and the communities they represent. This inclusive representation broadens access to knowledge and fosters a sense of belonging among young adults.
2. Hip hop workshops and programs: Libraries can offer workshops and programs that harness the creative energy of hip hop, enabling young adults to explore various elements such as DJing, graffiti art, rap lyricism, beat making, and dance. These interactive experiences not only facilitate skill

development but also promote self-expression, confidence, and community building.
3. Hip hop events and performances: Libraries can become vibrant cultural hubs by hosting hip hop events, such as open mic nights, rap battles, dance showcases, and panel discussions with hip hop artists and scholars. These events create opportunities for young adults to engage with the larger hip hop community, fostering dialogue, inspiration, and mentorship.

CONTROVERSIES AND CONUNDRUMS SURROUNDING HIP HOP

Hip hop, like any other cultural movement, has not been immune to controversies and conundrums. Here are some notable issues that have sparked debates and discussions within the hip hop community and beyond: misogyny and gender stereotypes, violence and gang culture, cultural appropriation, materialism and consumerism, and homophobia and LGBTQ+ representation. These controversies and conundrums reflect the complexities within hip hop as an artistic expression and cultural movement. They serve as opportunities for dialogue, growth, and reflection. These issues are ripe for youth librarians to use in connection to various library programs, such as book clubs, poster sessions, artivism, and more.

In sum, hip hop is not merely a music genre; it is a dynamic cultural force that has the potential to revolutionize library services for young adults. By embracing hip hop culture as a valid point of knowledge building, librarians can widen their repertoire of practices beyond those bound up with white ways of knowing, amplify diverse voices, and create inclusive spaces where young adults can express themselves, explore their identities, and engage with knowledge in meaningful ways. Through hip hop collections, workshops, events, and digital literacy initiatives, libraries become catalysts for empowerment, social justice, and equitable opportunities. Let us seize the power of hip hop and transform library services into vibrant, relevant, and transformative spaces for all young adults.

DISCUSSION QUESTIONS

- What other cultural resources might young adult librarians employ to promote social justice and equity in young adult services?
- How does Kumasi's thesis on hip hop comport with Lee's on youth pop culture?

6

Social Workers in the Library

ENHANCING SERVICES TO YOUNG ADULTS

Shannon Crooks and Renate Chancellor

Library and information science professionals have focused on connecting users to information since the inception of the profession in the nineteenth century. However, it was not until the Great Depression that libraries started developing innovative programs to help people connect to social services, find employment, and retrain to enter the workforce (Jaeger et al., 2014). In 2009, the San Francisco Public Library became the first library in the United States to hire a social worker at the city's main public library branch (Shafer, 2014). This trend quickly spread throughout the country, and it is estimated that 55 social workers are currently embedded in public libraries nationwide (Benson, 2022). Given that there are approximately 17,454 public libraries in the United States (WordsRated, 2023) and patrons have a tremendous need for assistance coping with challenges in their everyday lives (Crabtree et al., 2023; Hill, 2016), there are not enough social workers in libraries to meet the high public demand. We argue that young adults can benefit from the transformative services social workers bring to the library.

There are librarians who do not mind performing this work, but others assert that social work is outside their skill set and that they did not anticipate carrying out these types of services when they went to library school. As a former social worker librarian and co-author of this essay, I have seen teens experiencing many of these crises in the library, and I can attest to the fact that many librarians are not comfortable providing these types of social services. I have seen the panic and apprehension library staff experiences during emergencies, which is one reason the debate among public librarians on whether they should engage in social work exists.

The title of social worker is not always used to describe those who carry out this type of work in the library. For example, when I worked at the Prince George's County Library in Maryland, my job title was public services specialist. In this role, I engaged in crisis management interventions, cultivated partnerships with community organizations, and identified resources within the community to better assist young adults with these types of challenges. Examples of other titles used are community health coordinator, youth and family services worker, and interventionist coordinator.

Many teens live in situations where they experience complex challenges that go well beyond the scope of traditional library services. Librarians may encounter young adults in crisis situations who are caregivers for family members or experiencing a medical emergency. However, some of the more common issues include mental health issues, substance abuse, and homelessness as well as socioemotional and socioeconomic issues. Three types of challenges that commonly occur in public libraries along with strategies for how these might be addressed are discussed in more detail below.

MENTAL HEALTH

Signs of teens experiencing mental health challenges may not always be apparent to young adult librarians. Teens may have anxiety, depression, or eating disorders or are physically harming themselves. Social workers are experts trained to observe human behavior and are able to recognize these indicators. Teens can also experience distress in their home environment, which can lead to secondary traumatic stress. Secondary traumatic stress occurs when a person witnesses a family member or close friend experiencing a crisis, which results in trauma. Absent parents or lack of parental guidance, financial hardship, food insecurity, and instability in housing can all contribute to these types of emotional strain.

The literature on teen mental health issues encourages librarians to provide resources and facilitate programs that promote coping mechanisms (Harris, 1973; Takahashi, 2016). Librarians are encouraged to build a rapport with teens to create a safe space so that they feel comfortable discussing their challenges. This may not always work because it can be difficult for teens to seek help when they are in mental distress or experiencing other trauma, but a social worker can assist with these issues because they have extensive knowledge, training, and experience in assessing, diagnosing, and providing treatment for mental health illness.

HOMELESSNESS

Homelessness is a growing concern in the United States. "On a given night, the number of homeless children is over 194,300—accounting for one-third

Shannon Crooks and Renate Chancellor

of all homeless people, according to the National Alliance to End Homelessness" (Hill, 2016). As a social worker librarian, I utilized external resources and organizations to help with the homeless population at the library. The most significant barrier I encountered was homeless shelters requiring state-issued identification (ID) for individuals to gain entry to the shelter. This is a difficult barrier because to obtain an ID, an individual must have a mailing address and homeless people are not able to meet this requirement. To help alleviate this barrier, I partnered with a social worker who specializes in working with the homeless population and had them come to the library weekly to provide homeless individuals with these services. This allowed patrons to speak with a social worker who had knowledge of resources for the homeless and who could also make referrals for patrons to receive additional services.

Before establishing partnerships and collaborations with local community organizations, you need to identify community issues by conducting a community needs assessment. Identifying the challenges in your library community can start with a web-based community demographic data tool. PolicyMap is a web-based database that you can use to access information about your community. Visit policymap.org to create a fee-based account to find out where homelessness exists in your community to develop strategies to help unhoused patrons. PolicyMap can be used to identify organizations with resources to help teens and their families. Librarians can use the information about these organizations to create community resource libguides. Social workers are critical to this collaborative effort because they have firsthand knowledge of resources in the community and can serve as a liaison between the patron and the organizations.

MEDICAL EMERGENCIES

Most organizations require full-time social workers to be CPR and first aid certified, but this is not a requirement for librarians. Since it is impossible to predict medical emergencies, having an experienced social worker in the library can ensure that the library will be prepared in the event of such emergencies. These professionals will be able to evaluate the situation, develop a strategy, and offer a solution quickly. Establishing relationships with teens and their parents is also an important part of social work because it could ensure that the parents' or guardian's contact information is readily available in the library card database.

CONCLUSION

Young adults can benefit tremendously from the transformative services of social workers in the library. These services offer significant benefits and opportunities to serve and meet teens where they are. Meeting young adults' information and social needs is at the core of social work and library practices.

However, many librarians are not comfortable providing these services, and libraries are constrained by budgets and cannot afford to provide a staff member with this expertise. If a library does not employ a social worker on its staff, it may be because they believe that having a social worker would not contribute to or improve the quality of youth services, or it may be because they are facing financial constraints. If a library doesn't have a social worker on staff, there are alternative approaches that can be employed to help teens. Creating partnerships, building relationships with teen patrons, and developing programs around crisis prevention are examples of ways that librarians can work with teens in the absence of a social worker.

We would be remiss if we did not underscore the opportunity for library and information science educators who teach foundational and public library courses to include in this critical emerging topic in their curriculum. It offers students real-life expectations of work in a public library and creates awareness of how social workers can transform traditional library services.

DISCUSSION QUESTIONS

- What outcomes might libraries seek in providing this service?
- How might libraries measure or define "success" for this service?
- What sources of factual information might libraries pursue in considering adding social workers to their service profile?

REFERENCES

Benson, D. (2022). Why your local library might be hiring a social worker. *NPR*. https://www.npr.org/sections/health-shots/2022/01/03/1063985757/why-your-local-library-might-be-hiring-a-social-worker.

Crabtree, L., Latham, D., Gross, M., Baum, B., & Randolph, K. (2023). Social workers in the stacks: Public librarians' perceptions and experiences. *Public Library Quarterly*, 1-26.

Harris, M. H. (1973). The purpose of the American public library: A revisionist interpretation of history. *Library Journal*, *98*, 2509–514.

Hill, R. A. (2016). Almost home: How public libraries serve homeless teenagers. *School Library Journal*. https://www.slj.com/story/almost-home-how-public-libraries-serve-homeless-teenagers.

Jaeger P. T., Gorham U., Greene Taylor N., Kettnich K., Sarin L. C., & Peterson K. J. (2014). Library research and what libraries actually do now: Education, inclusion, social services, public spaces, digital literacy, social justice, human rights, and other community needs. *Library Quarterly*, *84*, 491–93.

Shafer, S. (2014). *Nation's first library social worker helps give hope to the homeless*. KQED. https://www.kqed.org/news/10341088/nations-first-library-social-worker-helps-give-hope-to-the-homeless.

Takahashi, D. (2016, May 29). The calm before the storm: How teens and libraries can fight mental illness. *YALSA BLOG*. https://yalsa.ala.org/blog/2016/05/29/the-calm-before-the-storm-how-teens-and-libraries-can-fight-mental-illness/.

WordsRated. (2023). *Number of libraries in the US*. https://wordsrated.com/number-of-libraries-in-the-us/.

7

Youth-Centered Young Adult Services

COCREATED SPACES, EXPERIENCES, AND OPPORTUNITIES

Anthony Chow

MY PERSPECTIVE AND CONTEXT

As a father of three adult children, I want to especially dedicate this chapter to my beautiful oldest daughter—Alex. She has reshaped how I approach being a father and represents yet another example of why it is essential that we should all be largely human and user centered when aiming to serve/parent/lead others. Alex is short for Alexander, and she was Theresa's and my firstborn. For the first 22 years of her life, she was my only son. A son whom I poured all my fatherly expectations and dreams into. Fishing, sports, watching action movies, and all my own perceptions of what I should do to teach Alex how to become a "man." She was a talented baseball player, but like most things we tried together as father and son, she just didn't seem to fit; she just didn't seem to find any passion for the game. Unbeknownst to me, Alex was realizing that he felt trapped in a male body and was more comfortable as a young girl than a young man. I still remember the day she shared this with me. In fact, it was my reaction that became the big issue she worked on with her therapist. While unsure of whether this would become a permanent transition, we loved all our children equally and just wanted them to become more of who they were meant to be, so we grew to accept the loss of our only son and the addition of our third daughter. Life, and Alex, has taught me to love her in a different way, but I still feel guilty for the many years I parented her as *I wanted to*, rather than the way *she wanted and needed to be parented*. She ultimately confided in me that many of the things we did together she did because she knew that was what I wanted.

I share this personal story as a preamble and potential context for providing young adult library services. Within this context, libraries need to serve as safe spaces to explore, to find a sense of belonging, to be a diverse and flexible place to find answers, to go on adventures, to meet new friends, and to be a space and place that teens want to use versus one that we, as adults, think they would like to use. As a library and information science (LIS) professor and strategic planning consultant, young adult services and spaces have always been a challenge for most libraries with which I have worked. The most successful libraries typically had a youth advisory committee, which facilitated free-flowing, frequent communication and feedback regarding the services and resources teens wanted and valued.

It is critical to keep in mind that each library's potential young adult user base is going to be clustered geographically close by, especially if it is a public library. The majority of patrons that use a library are going to live within a five- to seven-mile boundary—the demographics and unique needs of young adults living within the radius of a library who are most likely to use that library must be understood to increase the likelihood of a young adult user and information provision match. In other words, young adults are more likely to use a space that meets their needs.

CHALLENGES AND OPPORTUNITIES— ALWAYS A CHICKEN OR THE EGG SCENARIO

As with other library services, there is also an unending conflict between young adult library usage and the resources a library will or should allocate. Should a library invest resources in a young adult program or services if it's not being utilized? One could argue that these resources might be better allocated to services that are in higher demand or that young adult services and programs are not utilized because the library failed to allocate sufficient funding to make them more attractive and useful to these users. To help address these "chicken or egg" questions, we can turn to the field of user-centered design, which posits a direct relationship between meeting users' needs and their willingness to utilize a space, service, or resources.

If you just build it, they may very well not come. If you cocreate and cobuild it with the users you intend to serve, success is much more likely. We don't know what we don't know. Can you imagine developing something that teenagers would like without their input? I remember developing a website for middle school girls, and in our focus group, they said they wanted "bright" colors and for the site to be "cool," but we failed to dive deeper into what exactly "bright" and "cool" looked like to a middle school-aged girl. Our initial version was a disaster because we had designed it solely from our own frame of reference and life view; it was way off the mark. What did those terms mean to us versus a middle school girl? It's quite evident that we never had a real chance of developing a website that they would like without their input at every step of the way.

A HUMAN- AND USER-CENTERED DESIGN PERSPECTIVE

The general process for human-centered design (HCD) or user-centered design (UCD) is to involve the users you intend to serve throughout the design, development, implementation, and evaluation or assessment life cycle of any service, system, or technology. From my work as a strategic planner, I have learned that the people who use your library are going to be close by, which means you must talk to your local community members to understand their demographic makeup and unique characteristics. I have found that there tends to be trends in preferences based on various demographic variables, such as gender; race; and most definitely, age. You must keep talking to your community to try to understand what they want and/or need.

From a librarian's standpoint this means the following:

1. Putting together a representative advisory committee of young adults who live near your library (no more than 20–25 minutes away by car) that is diverse and reflects local demographics.
2. Asking the advisory committee to identify a list of their highest-priority information needs on a day-to-day basis. (Note: Do not ask them how the library can best serve them but rather what is important to them because they do not know all the ways in which a library can serve them.)
3. Supplementing the advisory committee's list with other data sources and then creating a rank-ordered list of highest priorities—ideally something in the 1 to 10 range.
4. Creating an ideal teen space that considers your top-10 list and other national/global young adult trends. The general rule in user-centered design is that you want to cocreate with users, although they are not library experts and will not know some of the ways a library can best serve them. You are the library expert, so your perspective and input will be invaluable.
5. Paying attention to architectural features that are fixed, so you also want to gather some data on these aspects of the space.
6. Keeping the advisory committee involved as potential designs are put forth and having them help with the color, signage, etc. An authentic teen perspective can be provided only by teens, so it's important not to try to anticipate what they want. Imagine how much has changed since you were a young adult?!
7. Inviting the advisory committee to provide feedback, with an eye toward continual improvement, when the space opens. Be sure to triangulate data to show that you are measuring the "success" of your young adult space and services from multiple sources—circulation, usage, attendance, and your advisory group feedback.

8. Consistently seeking opportunities to enhance, streamline, and adapt the space and services in response to teen input and advancements in technology, information availability, and other factors.

SERVING YOUNG ADULTS—A PSYCHOLOGICAL PERSPECTIVE

Jean Piaget, classifies young adults as being in their fourth stage of cognitive development—the formal operational stage—where adolescents are forming and testing hypotheses about themselves and the world around them (Malik & Marwaha, 2023). Erick Erickson posited that young adults are also in a stage of development called identity vs. role confusion, which means young adults are trying to define themselves based on how they compare to everyone else (Bernard, 1981). Major decisions they must make during this time concern physical appearance, dress, sexuality, hobbies, career choices, and popularity. It is a very anxiety-filled time, and libraries can certainly help young adults by providing a safe, objective, and highly robust set of resources to help them as they try to figure things out. Keep in mind my own personal story—libraries provide diversity and entire new perspectives that extend beyond a young adult's family, parents, culture, friends, school, and societal norms in general.

I remember a young adult focus group I led, where the teens told me the library was the safe place for "nerds" and the displaced. They said that teens who did not play sports or were not part of any club often used the library as a place to gather and stay safe from bullying and harassment. Also, since the school day typically ends before the average workday, a few teens said the library was a place where they could wait for parents to pick them up after work.

ASIAN AMERICAN/NATIVE HAWAIIAN/PACIFIC ISLANDER (AANHPI) AND UNDERREPRESENTED YOUTH-CENTERED LIBRARIES

The library is a place where young adults can learn about and be exposed to different people, cultures, and ideas. It is also a place for vetted, peer-reviewed, and high-quality resources. For the underrepresented or the nonmajority, it means that the library may be one of the few places where they can learn about different people and ideas outside of stereotypes, entertainment, and multimedia. For example, because of heightened geopolitical tensions involving China and Asia, coupled with a significant rise in xenophobia directed at Asians/Asian Americans caused by the pandemic, libraries have assumed a more critical role as sanctuaries and sources of a more comprehensive and equitable perspective for the AANHPI community. Bringing teens into this equation, especially within the context of the diverse and often less supervised school environments, reveals a troubling reality. Aside from the more widely covered cases of violence and racial discrimination against AANHPI individuals, instances of bullying; racial discrimination; and the use of slurs in school settings, such as hallways, parking lots, and gyms, are rampant and frequently unreported.

This is, unfortunately, not unique to the teenagers—any noticeable or significant difference can lead to an individual's being singled out; belittled; and in general, made to feel uncomfortable about their identity. For young adults in the AANHPI community, libraries as places where they can share their experiences and access resources within safe, neutral, secure, and objective spaces are extremely important. Libraries are where these young adults can read about the sadness and anger caused by discrimination and understand that they are not alone in these experiences and that being AANHPI means that they are different but that they should also be on the same path as everyone else. A path that leads to a healthy identity, the freedom to pursue who they are meant to be, and the understanding that differences better define who they are—not inferior or "less than" simply because they do not see themselves in books, the media, or on big and small screens.

FINAL THOUGHTS

As a field, we must try to understand the appropriate context for providing young adult services in libraries. Adolescence is a busy time with lots of transitions. Young adults are often bombarded with lots of different activities that demand their attention (e.g., homework, work, and hobbies). Given the unique demands on this age group, it may be unrealistic to even expect that young adult services will ever be as popular as children or adult services. Nevertheless, following a user-centered approach can certainly improve young adult services, thereby increasing user satisfaction and library use by this group. This means meeting young adults where they are and providing the programming, resources, spaces, and services that truly meet their needs. In the end, this aligns with the fundamental purpose of libraries—to serve everyone, regardless of background, financial status, or origin. Libraries stand ready and waiting to serve.

DISCUSSION QUESTIONS

- What other approaches to envisioning young adults might libraries draw upon other than "developmentalism"?
- How does this author define "safe space"?
- How might libraries defend themselves if something negative happens in "safe spaces" defined like this?

REFERENCES

Bernard, H. S. (1981). Identity formation during late adolescence: A review of some empirical findings. *Adolescence, 16*(62), 349-58.

Malik, F., & Marwaha, R. (2023). *Cognitive development*. National Library of Medicine. StatPearls Publishing. https://www.ncbi.nlm.nih.gov/books/NBK537095/.

8

That Was Then. This Is Now. Not So Different.

PROGRAM EVALUATION AND YOUTH LIBRARIANSHIP

Melissa Gross

In the early 1990s, when I was a Master of Library and Information Science (MLIS) student preparing for a second career, one of the things my dear professors drummed into me was the ever-growing need for program and service evaluation. The need for evaluation was tied to the vulnerability of libraries in seeking public funds and the ongoing problem of public lack of knowledge about the role of librarians and libraries in the life of communities, issues that are still very much with us today.

At the time, output measures were being promoted in American library publications as a uniform, systematic way to quantify library services, compare one library to another, and talk about achievements and fiscal needs. In the course of my education, one of my professors, Virginia Walter, published two books on output measures targeted to children and young adult librarianship (1992, 1995). As a budding researcher, always interested in finding out what works and why, these methods were very attractive to me.

When I earned my MLIS and started working on my PhD, I also took a job as a children's reference librarian at a large public library. While I don't remember any across-the-board attempts to gather output measures (I have read about harnessing the whole library to collect data over the course of an "average" week of activity), there were many aspects of our work that we routinely kept track of that would be best described as output measures. For instance, I kept a hand tally of the reference questions I transacted. We had an automated circulation system and used the data housed in that system for collection development and weeding activities. We also kept excellent records of how many people showed up for our programs (e.g., storyteller performances, children's readers' theater, toddler story times, and baby lap sits). There was no separate young adult department or programming that I remember. Young adults moved pretty fluidly from the children's room to the adults' room and back again, depending on their preferences and needs. Our summer reading program was our major undertaking every year, and we paid close attention to how many young people participated, how many books they read, the prizes they won, and attendance at the end of the summer party. All of these numbers were reported up the chain of command, and while I can't attest to everything that went into the formulations of budgets, our department was very well funded. We never questioned why we were providing our services and programs. We never asked what these programs and services meant in the lives of attendees from the perspective of the people we served. Our excellent work seemed self-apparent. We trusted that all the librarians on staff were information professionals using their professional judgment to help young people develop a love of reading and to launch them on the road to lifelong learning.

By the time I had earned my PhD and began my work as an assistant professor, the world of program and service assessment had begun to evolve. The nature of quantitative assessment was beginning to be critiqued by many funding agencies as providing only a partial picture of the impact of sponsored interventions. People who receive support for projects normally have to provide reports detailing their successes and challenges, which funding agencies can, in turn, use to demonstrate how well their dollars are being spent. However, success described in terms of the number of people attending a program just doesn't tell the whole story. Funders wanted to know what these programs and services meant to the people who received them. They were interested in knowing what the impact (if any) was on their lives and whether anything changed for them resulting from their participation. While output measures help answer questions like how much or how many, outcome measures focus on a program's ability to produce the desired change in areas such as knowledge, skill, behavior, attitude, or social status. Program benefits, described by participants, are a powerful way to illustrate the impact of the resources used to support them. To respond to the need for this kind of information, an approach called *outcome evaluation* was introduced by many nonprofit agencies, including the United Way and the Institute for Museum and Library Services (IMLS).

In 2000, when I received my first IMLS grant with co-principal investigator Eliza Dresang and the St. Louis Public Library, outcome evaluation was required of grant recipients. As a result, our study, which was among the first to assess children's in-library computer use beyond observing whether the computers were being used (a kind of output measure) to paying attention to what the children were doing on the computers (Dresang et al., 2006), incorporated outcome-based planning and evaluation into our research protocol. We developed the CATE (Children's Access to and Use of Technology Evaluation) OBPE (Outcome-Based Planning and Evaluation) model to guide our study of children's (aged 11–13) computer use in public libraries and included the voices of youth in our evaluation.

At the time of this writing, I have been teaching research methods for 25 years. Not research methods in the sense of how to use a database, but rather, research methods regarding how to create new knowledge, how to find out when the literature you read doesn't fully answer your questions, and how to evaluate library programs and services. I teach research methods because I love the subject and want students not only to love it but to be excited about using it to enrich their professional lives. I am proud of my school for including research methods in the curriculum. Not all schools do, and I believe it gives our students an advantage in the workplace. I hear from many librarians that evaluation seems complicated and difficult and they lack confidence in their ability to assess programs and services. To help with this, I have written a lot about program and service evaluation; given many workshops; and with my co-authors, produced two books specifically for youth librarianship on outcome-based evaluation (Dresang et al., 2006; Gross et al., 2022) as well as one on outcome-based evaluation in public libraries (Gross et al., 2016) and one on assessing digital reference services (McClure et al., 2002).

Many libraries are still collecting key output measures and finding them useful. Automation has helped make some data immediately and continuously available, such as circulation statistics and digital reference transcripts. Still, I am aware that many professionals across many fields (not only in library and information science [LIS]) shrink from the evaluation task. While I have not performed systematic pragmatic research on this phenomenon, I do have some ideas, many of which you will find others have written about, too, in considering why evaluation still is not routinely and universally used to plan and assess youth programs in public libraries and why the voices of users are often left out of the program design, delivery, and evaluation processes.

WHAT'S THE PROBLEM WITH EVALUATING LIBRARY PROGRAMS?

The original logic handed to me by my professors still stands in many ways. Librarianship is a profession. It requires a graduate degree where we are taught specialized knowledge. This degree is normally augmented by on-the-job training. We know what we are doing, and there isn't a strong tradition in youth librarianship of evaluation. Further, since many LIS schools do not teach research methods or program and service evaluation, it is not uncommon for graduates to take jobs in libraries where program and service evaluation is not part of the culture or not fully incorporated into professional activities. I have been told by some that a person interviewing for a library job might actually be disadvantaged if they demonstrate strong research skills. This perspective really surprised me. There is a perception that librarians who lack training in empirical research may be afraid of revealing this in the context of their work and/or may be afraid of confronting their lack of skill by seeking further education, especially if their employer is not bringing it up.

After all, evaluation can seem like just one more thing to do in an already very full agenda, and the payoff for putting in the effort may not be apparent. It takes some effort to produce the needed data, and if the effort isn't powered by a true desire to know and/or isn't valued by the chain of command, the motivation to evaluate may be difficult to generate. It helps a lot if the effort is supported by management and it is made clear what happens to the data, that is, who gets to see it and how it is used to leverage the amazing work the library is doing.

Following from this is the idea that if program and service evaluation skills are not required by the employer or by a funding agency or this data is not asked for by the public, such evaluation is unlikely to occur. What happens, though, when questions are asked about programs and we do not have the data to respond? Some librarians may rely on the scant literature on youth services program evaluation that exists or take to what is called "fake knowing," using the secondhand understandings they hear others use or conclusions based on their own unsystematic observations.

I do not believe that this is what the profession wants. The truth is that professional opinion is not a stand-in for data. Indeed, there have been many attempts to help librarians gain skills in planning and evaluation and to simplify the process. I do like to think that an attitude of curiosity or a desire to understand the impact we are having on youth motivates many professionals to ask important questions about their efforts. In addition to my own work, librarians interested in learning more can access these resources:

- Connected Learning Lab Research Tools: https://connectedlearning.uci.edu/research-tools/
- Evaluation Guide for Public Libraries: https://www.urbanlibraries.org/files/KHG-Evaluation-Guide.pdf
- Project Outcome: https://www.ala.org/pla/data/performancemeasurement
- YALSA Teen Services Evaluation Tool: https://www.ala.org/yalsa/sites/ala.org.yalsa/files/content/guidelines/yacompetencies/evaluationtool.pdf

Librarians may also consider courses offered through multitype library cooperatives or reaching out to LIS schools to get expert guidance and partners in research.

WHAT WILL WE GET IF WE DO EVALUATE?

One of the things we learned on Project CATE was that the introduction of systematic planning and evaluation will change your (professional) life. This may be hard to conceptualize if you have never experienced it. At the St. Louis Public Library, we saw improved relationships between users and staff because asking people about their experiences with the library tends to generate good-will. External stakeholders and the youth in the community experienced an enhanced understanding of how the library contributes to the welfare of youth as well as an increased demonstration of the library's responsiveness to the needs of young people.

At the same time, staff perceptions of their work and role in the community changed in that they became more goal oriented. It was clearer to everyone what they were trying to achieve, not just in a specific program, but in their day-to-day work and interactions with the public. Interdepartmental relation-ships were strengthened because the part each played in reaching specified goals and their contributions to desired outcomes were shared with everyone. The process made the value of assessment clear, and people appreciated having understandable feedback that allowed them to be innovative in making improvements. Note that even though this library was already innovative and committed to excellence in programming, the incorporation of systematic plan-ning and evaluation was an experience that enhanced the good work the library was already doing and helped bring this good work to the attention of the city government and the public.

When we know what it is we are trying to achieve in our work and have the data to demonstrate our successes and challenges, it allows us to make the case for funding and other kinds of support. We can leverage our important work by sharing what we learn with funders, partners, library administrators, managers, governing bodies, and the community. We can also be sure that li-brary staff members know the outcomes of services so that they can recognize the value of their contributions, can be aware of the meaningful work being achieved, and can help advocate for the library in the community.

Evaluation helps us maximize our opportunities to do better by increasing our engagement with our work and making our work intentional. It helps us improve our professional skills and increase our value. I continue to believe that students who bring research and evaluation skills with them to the job market have an edge over the competition. While one research class is not enough to make someone a seasoned researcher, these students are prepared to meet the need for continuous improvements, engage users, and satisfy their own curiosity about the impact of their work. Research and evaluation skills provide a path for youth librarians to give voice to youth by making them partners in de-signing and understanding the impact of programs and services. It strengthens the relationship between the library, its partners, and the community at large.

CONCLUSION

I believe that there is much professional and personal satisfaction to be gained from the design, delivery, and evaluation of programs and services that are intentional. The ability to speak of the impact of these programs and make program improvements based on authentic data is a critical skill for youth librarianship. Evaluation is something I will continue to teach and promote as an LIS educator. However, while I see the value of systematic evaluation so plainly, I also see that the path to normalizing the evaluation of all programs and services as standard professional practice is a difficult one. This is something I see our profession continuing to promote and trying to facilitate, yet after all these years, I don't think program and service evaluation will be normalized until it is mandated and becomes an integral part of library culture. This is something the IMLS and other funding agencies have tried to effect by requiring evaluation as a condition for grant recipients, but that only goes so far. This is something the ALA and several of its divisions continue to promote. Change continues to be hard to achieve.

DISCUSSION QUESTIONS

- After having read this essay, how would you pitch the idea of regular program evaluations for a library program that does not use them?
- How can program evaluations help youth librarians in catering to their often unique user base?
- What are some reasons libraries might oppose systematic outcome measures?
- What are some strategies and techniques for overcoming opposition to evaluating young adult services based on outcome measures?

REFERENCES

Dresang, E. T., Gross, M., & Holt, L. E. (2006). *Dynamic youth services through outcome-based planning and evaluation.* American Library Association.

Gross, M., Mediavilla, C., & Walter, V. A. (2016). *Five steps of outcome-based planning and evaluation for public libraries.* ALA Editions.

Gross, M., Mediavilla, C., & Walter, V. A. (2022). *Five steps of outcome-based planning and evaluation for youth services.* ALA Editions.

McClure, D. R., Lankes, D. R., Gross, M., & Choltco-Devlin, B. (2002). *Statistics, measures, and quality standards for assessing digital reference library services: Guidelines and procedures.* ERIC Clearinghouse. https://files.eric.ed.gov/fulltext/ED472588.pdf.

Walter, V. A. (1992). *Output measures for public library service to children: A manual of standardized measures.* American Library Association.

Walter, V. A. (1995). *Output measures and more: Planning and evaluating young adult services in public libraries.* American Library Association.

Part Two

Intellectual Freedom and Collections

9

Challenges and Opportunities in Young Adult Collection Development

Michael Cart

The field of young adult collection development is currently replete with both challenges and opportunities. Chief among the challenges—by both local persons and national organizations—is the nearly unprecedented spate of attempts to censor and ban young adult books. As for opportunities, happily, the present golden age of young adult literature provides myriads of those for selecting, acquiring, and enriching collections with exemplary titles.

Charles Dickens might well have had all of this in mind when he wrote his famous words, "It was the best of times; it was the worst of times," for—in terms of the best—there are, as we will see, abundant opportunities informing and enriching the field of young adult collection development. On the other hand, however, there are currently challenges that by far, exceed the available opportunities. In that regard, it is, indeed, the worst of times. What, specifically, are these opportunities and challenges?

CHALLENGES IN YOUNG ADULT COLLECTION DEVELOPMENT

What better place to start to answer that question than with the explosion of book challenges plaguing both school and public librarians. The number of challenges they must deal with has been growing exponentially. Consider that in 2021, the American Library Association's (ALA) Office for Intellectual Freedom (OIF) recorded 729 book challenges, then a new record. By 2022, only a year later, the number had nearly doubled to 1,269, the highest number of attempted book bans since ALA began compiling data about censorship in libraries 21 years ago. In terms of unique titles targeted for censorship, 2,571 were selected, another record, a 38 percent increase over the 1,858 titles in 2021 (Garcia, 2023).

According to OIF author, Eric Stroshane (personal communication, April 3, 2023), a total of 58 percent of these reported challenges targeted school libraries, classroom libraries, or school curricula, while 41 percent targeted public libraries. The remaining 1 percent were at institutes of higher learning and other institutions. An understanding of the individuals or groups behind these challenges is instructive. The OIF reports that 34 percent of titles were challenged by pressure groups/religious organizations; 26 percent, by parents; 19 percent, by boards/administration; 9 percent, by public library patrons; 7 percent, by "other/unknown"; 3 percent, by librarians/teachers/staff; 2 percent, by elected officials; and 0 percent, by students (Eric Stroshane, personal communication, April 3, 2023).

Many may find that 3 percent by librarians/teachers/staff particularly disturbing since it smacks of self-censorship, a particularly insidious kind. It's surprising that there are no figures for publishers, who are equally guilty of self-censorship. The often-censored author Judy Blume had this in mind when she wrote, "It's not just the books under fire now that worry me. It is the books that will never be written. The books that will never be read. And all due to the fear of censorship. As always, young readers will be the losers" (Blume, 1992, as cited in Donelson & Nilsen, 1997, p. 392). Indeed, fear of censorship may increasingly become a factor. The Tennessee legislature passed a bill that would subject publishers and distributors to criminal prosecution and substantial fines for providing public schools with material that is deemed to be obscene.

As the number of challenges grows, their nature changes. Historically, a challenge was typically submitted by a single person (usually a parent) to a single book. Now, however, 90 percent of the challenges are for multiple removals and are organized by groups of national scope, although one person, Texas legislator Matt Krause, seems to have set a dubious record of sorts when in 2021, he submitted to the Texas Education Agency a list of 850 titles he wanted investigated because, he said, that they "might make students feel discomfort, guilt, anguish, or any other form of psychological distress because of their race or sex" (Krause, 2023, as cited in Haupt, 2023, para. 21). Students are surely not the only ones to experience psychological distress, however; imagine the feelings of the hard-pressed librarians who must find the time to examine the list and vet each title!

Meanwhile librarians and free speech advocates have lately noticed an increase in heavy-handed tactics, including high-profile political pressure against certain books and legal threats against librarians who are responsible for selecting reading matter and not only legal threats, it should be noted, but also threats of physical harm. In some areas, ALA reports, challenges are being backed by intimidation from local armed groups. In Idaho, for example, a local librarian resigned after a bullying campaign that included armed men standing in the back of board meetings. Librarians who reject book banning have been threatened, harassed, sued, fired, and labeled "groomers" and "pedophiles" on social media (Allam, 2023).

"What we're seeing right now is an unprecedented campaign to remove books from school libraries but also from public libraries that deal with the lives and experience of people from marginalized communities," says Deborah Caldwell-Stone, director of ALA's OIF (as cited in Harris & Alter, 2022a, para. 6). "We're being confronted with the potential for another McCarthy era where people's lives are ruined simply because of what they believe or who they are" (Caldwell-Stone, 2023, as cited in Allam, 2023).

It is significant, in this regard, that the majority of the challenges school and public libraries receive now focus on sexual orientation, gender identity, race, and racism. Consider that PEN America, in an April 2023 study, reported that of 1,477 book bans recorded, 41 percent feature LGBTQ+ content, 40 percent contain characters of color, and 21 percent contain issues of race and racism (Alter, 2023). For further evidence, consider the constituents of the ALA (Banned and Challenged Books, 2022) top-10 list of most challenged books in 2022. Not surprisingly, the top two most challenged books had LGBTQ+ content: first was Maia Kobabe's *Gender Queer: A Memoir*. Second was George M. Johnson's *All Boys Aren't Blue*. Five others were challenged for LGBTQ+ content. In order they are as follows:

4. Mike Curato's *Flamer*
5. John Green's *Looking for Alaska*
6. Stephen Chbosky's *Perks of Being a Wallflower*
7. Johnathan Evison's *Lawn Boy*
10. Juno Dawson's *This Book Is Gay*

Thus, more than half of the top 13 have LGBTQ+ content; three feature characters of color:

3. Toni Morrison's *The Bluest Eye*
8. Sherman Alexie's *The Absolutely True Diary of a Part-Time Indian*
10. Ashley Hope Perez's *Out of Darkness*

To round out the top 10, three were challenged for having explicit sexual content:

9. Ellen Hopkins's *Crank*
10. Jesse Andrews's *Me and Earl and the Dying Girl* (There was a four-way tie for 10th place.)

The challenging groups and organizations routinely describe themselves as defenders of parents' rights. Some work at the district and state level, and others have national reach. And over the last several years, they have grown vastly more powerful. According to PEN America, there are at least 50 groups across the country currently working to remove books. Some of these groups have seen explosive growth recently. Of the 300 chapters that PEN America tracks, 73 percent were formed after 2020 (Alter, 2023). Welcome *Brave New World*. Arguably, the most prominent among these groups is the Florida Citizens Alliance, established in 2013. The conservative group has a network of more than 250,000 people. According to founding member Keith Flaugh, they are focused on "education and letting parents decide what the child gets rather than having government schools indoctrinate *our kids*" (Flaugh, 2022, as cited in Harris & Alter, 2022b, para. 6). There are also several conservative advocacy groups, including No Left Turn in Education (which has chapters in 27 states); the Freedom Fighters; and Patriot Mobile Action, a self-described Christian cell phone carrier that has reportedly spent hundreds of thousands of dollars in Texas school board races in support of candidates with conservative views on race, gender, sexuality, and which books children should be able to access in school.

The Patriot Mobile Action committee's stated aim is to eliminate critical race theory and "LGBTQ indoctrination" from schools. Even books without sexual content can be problematic, the group asserts, if they include LGBTQ+ characters because these are "sexualizing children."

One of the other main organizing—and particularly insidious—engines that drive the new spate of book challenges is Moms for Liberty, a conservative non-profit group that was founded in Florida in 2021. Currently, it boasts about 250 chapters across 42 states. Tiffany Justice (note the ironic name), cofounder of the group, recently told *The New York Times* that she rejected the notion that her organization contributes to harassment campaigns against library workers, arguing the group has a "joyful warriors" code of conduct and would not take responsibility for bad actors. "I do not endorse any type of harassment tactics," she concluded, "but the truth of the matter is, if you have activist teachers or you have librarians that are acting in defiance of state law or federal obscenity law and they are keeping books in libraries, I do hope they get fired" (Justice, 2023, as cited in Allam, 2023, para. 18).

In addition to citizen groups, the government is also challenging the concept of intellectual freedom. For example, there are two bills, introduced in the Indiana state legislature, that aim to restrict what teachers can say in the classroom. As such, they prohibit teaching about race, sex, color, national origin, ethnicity, religion, LGBTQ+ issues, and politics. The bills would require classroom materials to be vetted by parent review committees and posted online. They would also eliminate the legal protections that permit school libraries to use learning objectives as justification for sharing what some consider "harmful material" with minors (i.e., material they deemed obscene, pornographic, or violent). The vagueness of these pieces of legislation could be used to silence protected speech on a multitude of topics and have historically been used to ban materials dealing with sex education and LGBTQ+ issues.

As a result, states and districts nationwide have begun to impose constraints on the materials and books that librarians can order. At least 10 states have passed laws giving parents more power to control which books appear on library shelves, limiting students' access. At the same time, school districts are passing policies that bar certain kinds of texts—most often those focused on issues of race, gender, and sexuality—while increasing administrative or parental oversight of acquisitions. To date, 25 states have also passed laws restricting what teachers can say about race, racism, history, sex, and gender.

The most famous, or infamous, piece of legislation that deals with these issues is Florida's notorious Parental Rights in Education Bill, commonly called, "Don't Say Gay." The bill stipulates that "classroom instruction by school personnel or third parties on sexual orientation or gender identity may not occur in kindergarten through grade three or in a manner that is not age-appropriate or developmentally appropriate for students in accordance with stated standards" (Florida House of Representatives, 2022, pp. 4–5). Obviously, the language ("age appropriate" and "developmentally appropriate") is vague; it could be applied to any grade. So it was no surprise when it was subsequently expanded to forbid classroom instruction on the topics of sexual orientation and gender identity in all grades, an expansion that did not require legislative approval. One can imagine the chilling effect these bills have had on classroom instruction. It is arguable that the true intent of the bills is to marginalize LGBTQ+ students and their families. Furthermore, one can also argue that these laws violate the constitutionally protected rights to free speech, equal protection, and due process of these students and families.

For instance, Natanson (2023) reports that in the Keller Independent School District (Texas), librarians are required to follow a specific process when ordering books. First, they must complete a Google form in which they identify any content that might be considered problematic, such as "passionate and/or extended kissing" or "discussion or depiction of gender fluidity." Once this is done, they must submit their selections to the school board for a 30-day public review. During this time, parents have the opportunity to examine, and potentially challenge, the proposed book purchases. Finally, the entire school board votes to either approve or reject each item on the list.

Rick Stevens, a Florida pastor who serves on a book-reviewing subcommittee of the Florida Citizens Alliance (see above), said school librarians should welcome the extra pairs of eyes, which he believes will lead to more "pristine" school libraries, stocked solely with texts devoted to the fundamentals of reading, writing, and arithmetic (Natanson, 2023). "Sexual issues and sexuality—our children don't need to be introduced to that. We don't have to feel a responsibility to provide every kind of material for students" (Stevens, 2023, as cited in Natanson, 2023, para. 10).

So what can individual librarians do should would-be censors visit their library?

BEFORE THE CENSOR COMES

It is imperative to be prepared before materials are challenged. Fundamental to such preparation is the adoption of a carefully thought-out materials selection policy, which guides the selection, acquisition, and deselection processes. Such a policy should include the adoption of such ALA-generated intellectual freedom documents as the Library Bill of Rights, Freedom to Read, Freedom to View, and the Interpretation of the Library Bill of Rights. It should also include or reference a materials reconsideration form. In that connection, the policy should also speak to the acquisition of potentially controversial materials. The Monroe County Public Library (Indiana) addresses that need as follows:

> The library's goal is to provide a diverse Monroe County community with materials that reflect a wide range of views, expressions, opinions and interests. Specific acquisitions may include items that are considered controversial and may offend some users. Inclusion of questionable language or attitudes in materials is not in itself a reason to exclude them from the collection. The Library's acquisition of these items does not constitute endorsement of their content but rather makes available its expression and supports the principle of intellectual freedom. (2023, para. 2)

Other constituents of a materials selection policy should include consideration of the library and its community, the scope of the collection, criteria for selection, collection maintenance (i.e., selecting, weeding, and replacing), and provision for community involvement/feedback.

It is increasingly important that the materials selection process include consulting and documenting reviews that have appeared in leading review media (e.g., *Booklist, School Library Journal, Kirkus Reviews, Horn Book*, and *BCCB*) prior to purchasing, to help confirm the viability of the material selected—and referenced should it be challenged.

Aside from policy, cultivation of community-wide support, prechallenge, is vital. For example, the Beverly Hills (California) Public Library boasts a 3,000-member Friends of the Library organization, which is active in its support of the library. And speaking of friends, it is a good idea to befriend representatives of the local press.

WHEN THE CENSOR COMES

Don't panic. Be welcoming. Communicate openness. Listen more than you speak. Practice active listening (e.g., "You obviously care about children a great deal"). Stay calm and courteous. Distribute facts, policies, and other background materials—in writing. Give a clear and nonintimidating explanation of the procedure for registering a complaint (usually a request for a title's reconsideration) and be clear about when a decision can be expected.

If all of this is fruitless—and in today's politically charged atmosphere it is likely to be—your friends in the local press should be alerted; they will help to make the situation as transparent as possible to spur community-wide support. And if local resources prove to be inadequate, don't forget there are national organizations that can help, notably ALA's OIF; PEN America; and if the challenge involves materials with LGBTQ+ content, there is LAMBDA Legal. You are not alone.

OPPORTUNITIES IN YOUNG ADULT COLLECTION DEVELOPMENT

In light of the nearly overwhelming number and types of challenges that infest the field, it is difficult to find the proverbial silver lining in the current dark cloud of controversy. But it is there if one looks closely enough. It is the fact that by all accounts, young adult literature is—in terms of both quality and quantity—in a new golden age, offering a veritable feast of opportunities for selection and acquisition. Ironically, at a time of nearly unparalleled challenges, particularly noteworthy in this connection are LGBTQ+ literature—also in a golden age— and graphic novels (GN), which are not in a golden but platinum age, according to Mark Siegel, founder of First Second books, arguably the preeminent publisher of GN. As for LGBTQ literature, its numbers alone are salutary. Consider that in 2017, a total of 74 books with LGBT+ content were published; in 2018, the number increased to 91; in 2019, to 143; in 2020, 176; in 2021, 192; and 2022 saw a dip with a total of 167. This dip may be a statistical anomaly or an indication that publishers are cutting back on the number of LGBTQ+ books in light of the rampant challenges such books are receiving. One hopes not, and happily, the news of 2023 is cause for optimism. As of June 2023, 100 titles with queer content have been published or scheduled for publication; at this rate, a total of more than 190 titles may be in the offing.

The quantity of these books is matched by the quality, which makes them highly worthy of consideration. For example, four out of the five 2021 National Book Award finalists featured queer content. The winner, *Last Night at the Telegraph Club* by Malinda Lo, was also selected as a Michael L. Printz Award Honor title. Graphic novels with queer content also deserve praise for their quality. Mariko Tamaki's *Laura Dean Keeps Breaking Up with Me*, for example, was a Printz Honor title; Mike Curato's *Flamer* is exemplary in its quality as is Maia Kobabe's *Gender Queer*, one of the most often banned young adult books in the United States.

Meanwhile, great strides are being made in the publication of books by and about BIPOC (Black, Indigenous, and People of Color) and other underrepresented people. Much credit for this must be given to the organization We

Need Diverse Books (WNDB), which—according to its mission statement—is a grassroots organization of children's (and young adult) book lovers who advocate essential changes in the publishing industry to produce and promote literature that reflects and honors the lives of *all* (emphasis added) young people.

Lastly, good news comes in the form of the results of a poll of 1,004 adults, conducted by Grinnell College and Seltzer and Co. Respondents were asked three questions about middle school library collections that were considered contentious or divisive because they explored sexuality, race, racism, and religion.

In response to the first question, which asked whether students should have access to books that address sexual orientation, racism, and gender identity, the respondents answered positively as follows: sexual orientation (56 percent), racism in the United States (76 percent), and gender identity (57 percent).

The second question asked who should play a role in deciding which books are selected for school library collections. A salutary total of 57 percent said school librarians; 55 percent said students, while 53 percent said families should as well. And in terms of oversight, 44 percent said that local elected school boards should be responsible, but happily only 17 percent said state elected officials.

A third question offered two options concerning views on controversial books. In reply, 62 percent expressed concern that materials of value to students could be removed from school libraries due to the current culture wars, while 30 percent were concerned that materials that were harmful to students would remain on school library shelves (Kirch, 2023).

In sum, then, we have seen—in widespread attempts to censor and ban young adult books—challenges to collection development. We have further seen how librarians can prepare to meet those challenges and finally, how a golden age of young adult literature offers myriad opportunities for expanding and enriching collections. It is, as Dickens presciently said, "the best of times and the worst of times."

DISCUSSION QUESTIONS

- Because the "golden age" of young adult literature currently concentrates on gender identity (LGBTQ+) and racial identity (BIPOC), are there other forms of identity (groups) also deserving of young adult collection protection?
- How might artificial intelligence (AI) affect issues of materials challenges and/or protection?
- If involving a library's local community in a formal collection development policy process, what happens when that local community is very conservative?

- How do you guarantee that your collections meet the interests and needs of your community?
- What can you do to prepare for the possible advent of a censor?

REFERENCES

Allam, H. (2023, March 4). Culture war in the stacks: Librarians marshal against rising book bans. *The Washington Post (Online)*. https://www.washingtonpost.com/national-security/2023/03/02/culture-war-stacks-librarians-marshal-against-rising-book-bans/.

Alter, A. (2023, April). Book bans rising rapidly in the U.S., free speech groups find. *The New York Times*. https://www.nytimes.com/2023/04/20/books/book-bans-united-states-free-speech.html.

Banned and Challenged Books. (2022). *Top 13 most challenged books of 2022*. https://www.ala.org/advocacy/bbooks/frequentlychallengedbooks/top10.

Donelson, K. L., & Nilsen, A. P. (1997). *Literature for today's young adults*. Longman.

Florida House of Representatives. (2022). *Parental Rights in Education*. CS/CS/HB 1557. https://www.flsenate.gov/Session/Bill/2022/1557/BillText/er/PDF.

Garcia, R. (2023, March 22). *Book challenges nearly doubled from 2021*. ALA Press Release. https://www.ala.org/news/press-releases/2023/03/record-book-bans-2022.

Harris, E. A., & Alter, A. (2022a, April 4). Book banning efforts surged in 2021. These titles were most targeted. *The New York Times (Online)*. https://www.nytimes.com/2022/04/04/books/banned-books-libraries.html.

Harris, E. A., & Alter, A. (2022b, December 12). A fast-growing network of conservative groups is fueling a surge in book bans. *The New York Times (Online)*. www.nytimes.com/2022/12/12/books/book-bans-libraries.html.

Haupt, A. (2023, June 9). The rise in book bans, explained. *The Washington Post (Online)*. https://www.washingtonpost.com/books/2022/06/09/rise-book-bans-explained/.

Kirch, C. (2023, March). National poll finds Americans support freedom to read. *Publishers Weekly*. https://www.publishersweekly.com/pw/by-topic/childrens/childrens-industry-news/article/91825-national-poll-finds-americans-support-freedom-to-read.html.

Monroe County Public Library. (2023, March). *Collection development policy*. https://mcpl.info/geninfo/collection-development-policy?gclid=EAaIQobChMIzl-rj2ZP1_QIVEMiUCROHOATHEAAYASAAEgL_BwE.

Natanson, H. (2023, January 22). Students want new books: Thanks to restrictions, librarians can't buy them. *The Washington Post (Online)*. https://www.washingtonpost.com/education/2023/01/22/students-want-new-books-thanks-restrictions-librarians-cant-buy-them/.

10

Self-Censorship in a Politically Charged Environment

Beth Brendler and Kerry Townsend

Censorship and the fear of societal retribution has been affecting information dissemination since ancient times. In Athens in 399 BCE, Socrates was condemned to death for the crimes of corrupting youth and religious heresy. In China, around 225 BCE, Confucian scholars were killed, and Confucian books burned because Confucian teachings were seen as contrary to the political beliefs of the Qin dynasty. The Index Librorum Prohibitorum (*Index of Prohibited Books*) was a list of books, published by the Catholic Church, that were considered heretical or ideologically dangerous. It was in use for over 400 years, until the mid-1960s. Such actions may lead authors to practice prior restraint, self-censoring the content they produce. The effects of such censorship can also be seen in textbooks, when publishers select the least objectionable content over the best materials. When librarians are faced with challenges to their professional selection decisions, it is tempting to avoid using or purchasing controversial materials. However, it is part of our professional ethics to provide materials for everyone in our service communities. Without a professional dedication to freedom of information, we cannot support a well-informed citizenry, which is the bedrock of our democracy.

Censorship, primarily about the legitimization and control of knowledge, is a constellation of practices ranging from active to passive. "Active practices include . . . redaction, restriction, relocation, and removal" (Knox, 2017, p. 269). While overt attempts to deny access to information are abhorrent, a much more insidious form of suppression of ideas, self-censorship, is a passive practice.

Self-censorship is the act of choosing to withhold information or ideas that may be controversial or offensive to some community members, based on personal values or fear of sanctions. Limiting access to information controls what is viewed as knowledge and truth, which reduces the availability of counter story-telling that challenges the dominant narrative.

A primary mission of libraries is to provide access to varied perspectives, in multiple formats, in a place accessible by all members of the community. Librarians should be proponents of the values of the profession, which holds intellectual freedom at the core. Self-censorship can limit access to information and ideas, create a climate of fear and intimidation, and undermine the role of the librarian as a trusted source of information. Information professionals may be responding to possible political and professional dangers, and in some cases, they are denying access to ideas they find personally problematic. This is not only undemocratic but also professionally unethical. Four of the American Library Association's eight principles in the *Code of Professional Ethics for Librarians* are related to equitable access to information and intellectual freedom.

Self-censorship can occur in any setting, but it is particularly worrisome in school libraries. When teachers or librarians avoid selecting good materials, specifically because they fear public reaction, they are self-censoring. This is the most dangerous type of censorship because it is largely invisible. When librarians opt to avoid purchasing or displaying potentially controversial materials, they may be responding to a perceived threat rather than an actual threat. The threat may be an assumption made based on their own value system or the political climate rather than an actual challenge.

In 2022, *School Library Journal* published their Controversial Books Survey. Ninety-seven percent of the school librarians surveyed reported that they weighed "the effect of controversial subject matter when making book purchase decisions" (Yorio, 2022, para. 23). The same survey reported that 88 percent of respondents had removed potentially controversial materials from their library, without a formal reconsideration, due to community inquiries.

In the light of that survey, consider the ramifications of recent challenges. In 2022, the American Library Association reported the highest number of materials challenges since it began compiling statistics on censorship. Prior to 2022, most challenges were attempting to restrict access to a single book. In 2022, 90 percent of the reported challenges were attempts to restrict multiple titles (Banned and Challenged Books, 2023, para. 4). This, and legislation that allows criminal prosecution of teachers and librarians for dissemination of "prurient" material and "divisive concepts" to children and teens, has made self-censorship in libraries and schools akin to self-preservation.

When librarians remove materials from their collections, it often limits the representation of nondominant groups. Books by and about marginalized groups, particularly LGBTQIA+ materials, are common targets for these challenges.

A notable feature of these challenges is an effort to frame any material with LGBTQIA+ themes or characters as inherently pornographic or unsuitable for minors, even when the materials are intended for children and families and they are age and developmentally appropriate. (American Library Association, 2020, p. 14)

Every child should have the chance to see themselves in what they read. The lack of representation creates "the single story" (Adichie, 2009) and leads children from the dominant culture "to view themselves and their lives as 'normal', to interpret their own cultural attitudes and values as 'human nature', and to view other people and other lives as exotic at best, and deviant at worst" (Bishop, 1997, p. 3). It also positions children from marginalized groups as invisible and secondary, not as valued members of the community. The Search Institute (2011) includes the community valuing youth and seeing children as resources as part of the 40 Developmental Assets "that help young people grow up healthy, caring, and responsible."

Another issue with self-censorship is that it can create a climate of fear and intimidation in the library. When youth patrons see that certain materials have been removed, they may be less likely to explore new ideas and topics. Self-censorship can also undermine the role of the librarian as a trusted source of information. When librarians remove materials from their collections, they are sending patrons a message that the library cannot be trusted to provide them with accurate and unbiased information. This can damage the relationship between librarians and children and teens and make it more difficult for them to do their job.

There are multiple ways to self-censor, such as avoiding purchase of potentially problematic materials, trigger labeling materials, keeping materials out of displays and off recommended lists, or moving children's and teens' items to the adult section. This is all done without a proper reconsideration procedure. The problem with labeling is that what might trigger one person might be self-affirming to another. In addition, the library professional implies that they have read, heard, or viewed all the items in the collection and have selected only the labeled items as "triggering" or "unsuitable." This gives patrons a false sense that someone is verifying library materials based on some standard value system. We must ask whose value system is the one on which decisions should be based? Who decides what a community values?

Library and information science students often ask whether the process of materials selection is an act of self-censorship because librarians are rejecting some materials over others. In 1953, Lester Asheim wrote about the difference between selection and censorship. His article remains relevant today. He noted that the basic difference is that the selector looks for values, strengths, and virtues that will overshadow minor objections. The censor, on the other hand, is looking for reasons to reject the materials. Their guiding principle leads them to seek out the objectionable features, the weaknesses, and the possibilities for misinterpretation (Asheim, 1953).

Choosing not to purchase materials because there are better treatments of the topic, the library already has a large, representative collection on the subject, or the collection management plan excludes certain materials from the library's scope is not censorship. It is selection and proper stewardship of library funds. It is when librarians choose not to select good materials because they might cause controversy or conflict with the values of some groups in the community or are counter to one's personal values, then self-censorship occurs.

In a politically charged atmosphere it can be difficult to create and follow collection management policies when the definitions of "obscene," "prurient," and "explicit sexual materials" are so unclear, even when defined within the context of state law or proposed legislation. Often librarians would rather err on the side of safety than risk their livelihoods on materials that might be problematic in the future. In addition, collection management policies do not provide protection from internal selection bias. This is why selection parameters must be explicit and publicly available.

There are several strategies that can be used to address self-censorship in libraries. One is to provide librarians with training on intellectual freedom issues and professional ethics. This training can help librarians understand the importance of providing access to a wide range of information, even if that information is controversial. Another is to develop strong, unambiguous policies and procedures that support intellectual freedom. Policies should include selection methodology, the parameters for selection, a clear collection scope, and information on reconsideration procedures and define who has the ultimate responsibility for collection management. The library mission should include or reflect the American Library Association *Library Bill of Rights* and *Freedom to Read Statement* or the National Council of Teachers of English *Students' Right to Read* and state that all members of the community have the right to access information. Library staff should make decisions based on the library's mission, values, and goals as well as their collection management policies. Other than regular collection maintenance, materials should not be removed from the collection without a formal reconsideration procedure.

It is important to create a climate of openness and trust in the library. This is particularly important in youth services, where children and teens are exploring their identities and beginning to develop empathy, respect for others, and social awareness. Self-censorship stifles free speech, limits access to information and ideas, and undermines the trust that librarians have built with their patrons. As a librarian supporting intellectual freedom, an understanding of the dangers of self-censorship is an essential part of professional ethics and practice.

Beth Brendler and Kerry Townsend

DISCUSSION QUESTIONS

- Think of a past work experience where you may have self-censored. What could you have done to combat this or what did you do?
- Many controversial topics can mean vastly different things to different people. How could this make avoiding self-censoring in youth librarianship more difficult?
- Discuss the challenges faced by librarians in defining and navigating "obscene," "prurient," and "explicit sexual materials" in collection management policies. How do these vague definitions contribute to self-censorship?
- As an exercise, develop a list of reasons to advocate for/against self-censorship?
- How might a young adult librarian engage young people in developing a collection development policy that protects their right to access library materials?

REFERENCES

Adichie, C. N. (2009, July). The danger of a single story [Transcript]. TED Conferences.

American Library Association. (2020). *The state of America's libraries 2020: A report from the American Library Association.*

Asheim, L. (1953). Not censorship but selection. *Wilson Library Bulletin, 28,* 63–67.

Banned and Challenged Books. (2023, March 20). *2022 book ban data.* http://www.ala .org/advocacy/bbooks/book-ban-data.

Bishop, R. S. (1997). Selecting literature for a multicultural curriculum. In V. J. Harris (Ed.), *Using multiethnic literature in the K-8 classroom* (pp. 1–19). Christopher Gordon.

Knox, E. J. M. (2017). Opposing censorship in difficult times. *Library Quarterly, 87*(3), 268–76.

Search Institute. (2011). *40 Developmental assets.* https://www.search-institute.org /downloadable/Ann-Arbor-Handout-2.pdf.

Yorio, K. (2022, September 8). Censorship attempts will have a long-lasting impact on school library collections, SLJ survey shows. *School Library Journal Online.* https://www.slj.com/story/censorship-attempts-will-have-a-long-lasting-impact -on-school-library-collections-slj-survey-shows.

11

Built in the Built Environment

LEVERAGING SOCIAL CONTROL IN CREATING AUTHENTIC
PUBLIC LIBRARY TEEN SPACES

Shari Lee

Teens are often monitored, controlled, and in many instances, excluded from using public spaces (Barrett, 2021). Consequently, teens usually "have no obvious rights to public space, and their ability to access landscapes and nature is often more restricted today than in previous generations" (Brunelle et al., 2018, p. 362). In this context, the need for public library teen spaces is undeniable. Calhoun (2020) speaks to the value of these spaces:

> Designated young adult spaces, often called "teen zones," aim to create space for adolescents to socialize, read, and engage in activities that support their developmental needs. Teen zones are critical for young adult services in public libraries, as, otherwise, adolescents may feel unwelcome in public libraries due to institutional policies such as no talking or eating and a lack of designated study spaces. (para. 1)

It is, therefore, exceedingly important that the spaces created for teens in public libraries function to legitimately serve their needs. They cannot be teen spaces in name only. In other words, they must function as *authentic* spaces for teens.

Even when public spaces are created specifically for teens, they often function to restrict, confine, or keep teens away from spaces frequented by adults. For example, Brunelle et al. (2018) find that skate parks often exemplify this strategy. On the surface, the construction of a skate park might appear to cater to the needs of teens by providing them a space for physical activity and social interaction. However, the creation of such venues often coincides with new regulations that limit or even forbid skateboarding in other public areas.

Consequently, skateboarding becomes confined to designated spaces, thereby limiting the likelihood of adults encountering skateboarders, also making it easier for teens to be monitored. These skate parks do not genuinely function as authentic teen environments because they exist primarily to monitor and control teen activity while favoring adult needs.

Tactics such as these occur primarily because of society's enduring negative perceptions of teens as rebellious, emotionally unstable, and inevitably prone to antisocial behavior. Researchers have framed this as a kind of demonization of teens that flourished once Hall (1904) identified adolescence as a separate developmental stage of life. Although Hall brought attention to adolescence as a thing, he is also the reason adolescence quickly evolved from thing to disease. The cure, as all diseases require a cure, was to control teen activity/behavior during this developmental stage. While these negative notions of adolescent development were fully discredited in the 1930s, the perception of the unruly, ill-behaved, and antisocial teen has persisted to this day. Sadly, many adults believe that these ideas of teens are inevitable and unavoidable aspects of teen development. It would be naïve to believe that this thinking has eluded libraries (i.e., non–young adult librarians, library staff, and library users).

This raises the question, how do these negative perceptions of teens affect the way public library teen spaces are designed and subsequently, how teens use and behave within these spaces? This is a critical question because humans have been shown to "alter or regulate their behaviors . . . with reference or deference to the built environment" (Manzo, 2005, p. 84). The built environment comprises all man-made structures in our surroundings. Simply stated, it is *man-made shelter* in all forms. The built environment has been of interest across disciplines, where researchers have been concerned with built forms, the spaces they enclose, the spaces they define, and the impact these have had on humans and human behavior for decades. Manzo (2005) believes that architectural features of planned spaces and the design elements (e.g., furniture, flooring, and lighting) can have a great effect on human behavior in a space because these features are also *players*, or *interactants*, in the space. He views this *effect* (intended or not) as a type of social control and suggests

> a broadening of the notion of social control beyond formal and informal human sources to include the physical features of spaces, spaces like shopping malls, and not only of prisons or similar institutions. This study advises that inanimate objects and the spaces that comprise them are informative for and relevant to behaviors of human interactants. (Manzo, 2005, p. 83)

Therefore, in Manzo's broader notion of social control, both planned spaces *and* design elements, such as furniture, can influence how humans behave in or use a space.

The fact that human behavior can be influenced by the built environment (planned spaces) indicates that Manzo's (2005) concept of social control can be deliberately utilized to elicit specific behaviors. This means that built structures, such as shopping malls, can be planned (designed) to "tell" humans how to use and/or behave within their boundaries (Semon, 2006). Simply understanding this relationship between individuals and the environment can be valuable to young adult librarians and beneficial to teen library users because social control, as it functions in the built environment, can be leveraged to enhance (or change) the library users' experience. As such, this understanding would be of value if considered when creating, designing, rebuilding, and rearranging public library spaces for teens.

The applicability of this to libraries is worth exploiting because city planners, architects, and designers have made and continue to make these types of adjustments regarding teens and the public spaces they use. These adjustments have included, for example, deliberately configuring benches in groups to encourage socialization and configuring them in a straight line to elicit the opposite outcome (Owens, 2002). This is why some say that public policies and zoning codes should take the needs, values, and opinions of adolescents into account and why they need to participate in decision-making processes. The thinking here is that this will generate healthier communities and encourage these future adults to be more engaged and responsible citizens (Passon et al., 2008).

Just as notions of teens have influenced the way other public spaces are created/designed, negative notions and/or biases regarding teens can also materialize in the physical aspects of a teen space. This alone is noteworthy, but when considered within the context of spatial design for purposes of social control, its significance cannot be overstated. The goal is to understand how social and cultural factors shape our interaction with planned structures and our behavior within the spaces they enclose. Ultimately, this will enhance our understanding of what makes a genuine and effective public library space for teens—one that genuinely accommodates teens and their needs and cultural practices. The expectation is that this will be beneficial to our understanding of the determinants of an authentic (i.e., successful) public library space for teens. An authentic public library teen space is defined here as one that accommodates teens and their cultural practices in a meaningful way (i.e., a teen space that facilitates teen use as determined by teens). This is best accomplished by including teens in the design process.

This aligns with Piazzoni's (2018) characterization of authenticity as the *dynamic interplay* that connects individuals, the spaces they occupy, and the significance attributed to those spaces. The author contends that when people engage with their environment or space, they incorporate moral, material, and symbolic dimensions, essentially formulating their own personalized interpretation of what constitutes authenticity within that particular spatial context.

Therefore, spaces hold diverse meanings for different individuals, signifying that the perception of authenticity can vary widely. This influences how individuals feel, behave, and relate to their surroundings, affecting both individual experiences and the broader societal dynamics within various spaces. Simply stated, an authentic space is one that people are able to use in the way that works for them—regardless of the creator's intent.

An authentic teen space would, therefore, function for teens as they wished, as opposed to functioning for the library, as many teen spaces have been created to do. These would be teen spaces in name only. Commenting on this issue 20 years ago, Bernier (2003) challenged libraries to build upon the legacy and advocacy of Samuel Swett Green by designing and redesigning libraries that respond to teens' cultural needs and ways of being, just as libraries have historically designed and redesigned services to respond to other cultural changes. Many libraries force teens to use the library as the institution dictates, which he contends often goes against teens' natural way of doing things; instead, he says, libraries should consider teens' cultural needs and ways of doing things when serving this demographic. Fifteen years later, Bernier (2018, as cited in Lange, 2018, para. 14) finds that "spatial inequality remains" because teens are still often excluded from the design process—or adults mistakenly believe that simply labeling a space makes it young adult.

Considering what we now know about social control in the built environment (that it can "tell" individuals what to do, e.g., Semon, 2006), spatial design and arrangement should be considered powerful tools in creating, re/designing, and re/arranging public library teen spaces. It is not simply what goes into the space that matters; the arrangement of design elements can have an even greater impact on how teens relate to the space. On the one hand, this could be deliberately used to enhance the users' experience within the space and to attract and retain users. On the other hand, if ignored or left to chance, it would have an inadvertent and random effect (i.e., positive or negative). Remember, social control is always present in the built environment in that we always orient ourselves to our environment (i.e., the built environment). The thing to keep in mind is that some people use (or harness) this knowledge to try to elicit certain or specific behaviors (i.e., to control social behavior in public spaces). Sometimes it works the way the creators intended, and sometimes it doesn't. Nevertheless, we will still respond to that "effort" in some way. Since social control is always present in the built environment, not brought about, it can be deliberately used (or harnessed) to influence behavior. If it is not deliberately used, then the effects are inadvertent or accidental, but there is still an impact.

Given that negative notions of teens (or biases) can be physically reflected and enacted in (built into) a teen space and our understanding of the tacit relationship between individuals and the built environment, the focus in teen space design must be expanded to include issues of social control in the built environment as well as how these intersect with negative notions of teens. The important lesson here is that you now understand how social control operates in the built environment, so you can choose to use it for good when creating or redesigning public library teen spaces. This is one tool you can use to ensure that the spaces you create for teens in public libraries function as authentic teen spaces.

DISCUSSION QUESTIONS

- How does the resurgence of youth curfew policies reinforce or contradict this author's thesis?
- In what ways might young adults be introduced into the library design (or renovation) process?
- What information sources might librarians use to discover model young adult library spaces?

REFERENCES

Barrett, E. J. (2021). *Defining their right to the city: Perspectives from lower-income youth.* Urban Affairs Forum. https://web.archive.org/web/20230201054331/https://urban affairsreview.com/2021/04/01/defining-their-right-to-the-city-perspectives-from -lower-income-youth/.

Bernier, A. (2003). YA space: The final frontier? In K. Worman (Ed.), *Young Adult Services Institute: Serving San Joaquin Valley teens in the 21st century* (pp. 163-77). San Joaquin Valley Library System.

Brunelle, S., Brussoni, M., Herrington, S., Matsuba, M. K., & Pratt, M. W. (2018). Teens in public spaces and natural landscapes: Issues of access and design. In J. E. Lansford & P. Banati (Eds), *Handbook of adolescent development research and its impact on global policy* (pp. 362-79). Oxford University Press.

Calhoun, E. (2020, Fall). Getting in the (teen) zone: Evaluating young adult spaces in public libraries through a user-experience framework. *iJournal: Graduate Student Journal of the Faculty of Information, 6*(1), 1-10. https://doi.org/10.33137/ijournal .v6i1.35267.

Hall, G. S. (1904). *Adolescence: Its psychology and its relations to physiology, anthropology, sociology, sex, crime, religion, and education.* (2 vols.). Appleton.

Lange, A. (2018, May). *Young adult architecture: Public libraries offer teenagers space where no one tells them to sit up straight or be quiet.* Curbed. https://archive.curbed .com/2018/5/24/17389648/library-architecture-teens-public-space.

Manzo, J. (2005). Social control and the management of "personal" space in shopping malls. *Space and Culture, 8*(1), 83-97.

Owens, P. E. (2002). No teens allowed: The exclusion of adolescents from public spaces. *Landscape Journal, 21*(1), 156-63.

Passon, C., Levi, D., & del Rio, V. (2008, September). Implications of adolescents' perceptions and values for planning and design. *Journal of Planning Education and Research, 28*(1), 73-85.

Piazzoni, M. F. (2018). Authenticity makes the city: How "the authentic" affects the production of space. In L. Tate & B. Shannon (Eds.), *Planning for authenticities* (pp. 154–69). Routledge.

Semon, K. (2006). Insidious design: The silent salesman and the American shopping mall. *Environmental & Architectural Phenomenology Newsletter, 17*(2), 8–10.

12

Challenges and Opportunities of the Misinformation Society

YOUTH LIBRARIANSHIP AS CONSCIOUS SOCIAL ACTION

Roger B. Pereira Domingues and Denise E. Agosto

Much has been written about the proliferation of inaccurate and misleading information online. Keyes (2004) suggested that the United States has reached a "post-truth era," where we find in the media not just factual statements and lies but a gray area between truth and fiction that includes statements falling just short of outright lies. Scholars across disciplines and national boundaries have identified many types of misleading messages shared online in the post-truth era, from politically charged "fake news," to hate speech, to unintentional factual errors shared over and over again by unwitting actors. In the US library and information science (LIS) literature, we typically define "misinformation" as any inaccurate or misleading information and "disinformation" as the subset of misinformation designed to be deliberately misleading (e.g., Agosto & Olt-mann, 2022). With this essay, we consider how those working in youth services can help young people identify and challenge misinformation and disinforma-tion from a socially conscious professional perspective intended to reveal the underlying social forces that give rise to and perpetuate misinformation.

Misinformation affects human decision-making and democratic participa-tion, whether it's at the individual level in relation to personal decisions, such as voting and health care; at the community level affecting decisions, such as local school curricula; or at the national level with determining influence on decisions as crucial to national well-being as joining or vacating economic blocks (e.g., false information campaigns in the lead-up to the Brexit vote in Great Britain). Some scholars trace the recent escalation of misinformation and resulting post-truth era to widespread public distrust of scientific and academic thought, coupled with a lack of interest in the veracity of information received and shared online (e.g. Araújo, 2021). Those at the extreme ends of public discourse tend to believe information that reaffirms their radical ideologies and reject information that contradicts their preexisting assumptions about the world, limiting their ability to weigh new ideas and perspectives.

People living in the post-truth era interact within a "misinformation society" characterized by individuals and organizations sharing misinformation within and across national boundaries. Teens and children who engage online will certainly encounter, live with, and have to deal with aspects of the misinformation society. Our emphasis in youth services should be on critical analysis of the social structures that give rise to misinformation and on developing ways to teach young people how to identify—and challenge—it.

CHALLENGES OF THE MISINFORMATION SOCIETY: EXAMPLES FROM THE UNITED STATES AND BRAZIL

The potential social harms of a misinformation society include weakening of democracy, the growth of authoritarianism and extremism, and the spread of a culture of hate. With much in common (and much in contrast) socially and politically, the United States and Brazil serve as useful examples of challenges and opportunities for LIS amid the rise of the misinformation society.

The 2016 election of Donald Trump is often used as a symbol of the post-truth era, as is the election of Jair Bolsonaro as Brazil's president two years later. Each rose to power on a populist, nationalistic platform. As political candidates and elected leaders both men used social media to gather support and refute opposition. Trump issued more than 57,000 posts on Twitter alone between 2009 and 2021, including thousands of misleading, unverifiable, and false statements. Similarly, Bolsonaro was "a master of social media," often using his accounts to share "explosive" content against LGBTQ+ people, women, and other oppressed groups (*The Economist*, 2019) as well as sharing COVID vaccine disinformation during the pandemic.

In both countries, the rapid spread of vitriolic and largely unverified online information was among the prime causes of violent political insurrection when each leader subsequently lost his bid for reelection. Groups of armed citizens led attacks on both seats of national government—on the US Capitol Building in Washington, DC, on January 6, 2021, and on the Three Powers Plaza in Brasilia on January 8, 2023. Eerily similar in nature, both armed revolts were organized largely through social media, and both fed on fears stoked by organized disinformation campaigns that sought to overturn fair elections. These events are part of "a broader crisis of trust" in information (Braga, 2023) that typifies the misinformation society.

These two examples together suggest a deconstruction of social values in the misinformation society and the surge of ethnocentric thinking, a worldview in which one or more privileged groups seeks to impose itself on others through violence, suppression, and disinformation. Although each example revolves around a single main figure, they both point to widespread sharing of misinformation by large groups of social media users who helped to stoke anger at election results and fervor for insurrection. Thus, the misinformation society is not merely synonymous with the circulation of false information, or even with the cognitive processing of information to support one's own biases (cognitive bias). Rather, it signifies a far-reaching, destructive culture that disvalues fact and a mentality that leads people to believe and share information without verifying it, even though it can be relatively easy to verify using simple online techniques (Araújo, 2021). Youth librarians must insert themselves into the political discourse to confront these political realities and work against this destructive culture and mentality.

We should note here that the idea of LIS as a politically neutral profession has long been debated in both the United States and Brazil. Brazil's "School without Party" movement ("Escola sem Partido," or "ESP") serves as a useful example of the danger of viewing public spaces and services, such as public and school library services, as neutral. We argue that "staying neutral" in our librarianship roles does not result in truly neutral services. Rather, a neutral stance means leaving misinformation unchecked and in fact, leads to its growth. As such, a neutral "hands-off" stance is actually favorable to the spread of disinformation.

The ESP movement was founded in 2004 by Brazilian lawyer Miguel Nagib ostensibly to curtail ideological indoctrination in Brazilian public schools. Nagib and other ESP organizers launched a social media campaign against perceived leftwing politicking by public school teachers. ESP organizers used social media to present emotionally charged vitriol as "fact" in support of their cause, calling on students to film their teachers discussing "partisan" issues in school, such as evolution or LGBTQ+ rights, and to post the videos on social media as a form of public shaming. Teachers across Brazil feared that any classroom mention of contemporary social issues could lead to public humiliation and job dismissal.

The ESP movement generated fear among public educators, augmenting long-standing educational inequities between well-funded private schools, where teachers could engage in unrestricted classroom dialogue, and lesser-funded public schools, where teachers feared retribution for teaching about contemporary social issues, despite legal requirements in Brazil's Constitution for equal curricula in public and private schools.

The ESP social media campaign gained national visibility and led to the eventual introduction of more than 50 local, state, and national bills aimed at making the discussion of "political" topics illegal in public schools (Ferreira & Souza, 2018). The majority of these bills have since been rescinded, largely in light of negative pushback from educators, human rights groups, and others opposed to the ESP's ideology.

Regardless, the popularity of the ESP reveals a troubling social effort to increase inequity in an already inequitable system. ESP movement leaders used carefully crafted social media posts to appropriate the words "politics" and "party" (as in "political party") to gain support for their campaign. It is only through examining the ESP's messages within the broader social context of Brazilian politics that the intentional distortion of language for emotional impact becomes clear as a way of amplifying inequality through the use of the state-sanctioned apparatus.

OPPORTUNITIES OF THE MISINFORMATION SOCIETY: LESSONS FROM PAULO FREIRE

Thus, the core LIS challenge of the misinformation society is to ensure the future of healthy public discourse. To meet this daunting challenge, we must adopt a socially conscious professional framework that acknowledges library services for young people as inherently political acts. Librarians are not just providers of information but also information educators (Agosto, 2018). As Brazilian education scholar Paulo Freire (2018) has argued, education cannot be divorced from the sociopolitical contexts in which it takes place. We must recognize that librarians' actions exist within sociopolitical contexts that imbue them with political meaning. Even simple library policies represent political statements, embodying the values of the librarians who write them and of the communities in which they are situated. For example, a sign in a teen room announcing "Quiet! People are reading," values the actions of teens engaged in reading over those using the library for social interaction space. It ignores the sociopolitical reality that teens who use libraries for social interaction are often members of oppressed groups who lack social power and sufficient resources to use other community spaces, such as restaurants and sports fields, for social interaction.

Even the physical placement of library buildings can embody social privilege and reify oppression. In the city of Belo Horizonte, within the state of Minas Gerais, Brazil, for instance, the main state public library building is within easy reach only for those who live in very wealthy nearby neighborhoods. Lacking a well-resourced branch library system, residents of lower socioeconomic groups across the huge state of Minas Gerais (larger in area than Spain!) must take lengthy bus rides to access library services. This design sends a message of exclusion to those with limited economic means and serves to further oppress groups that lack social power.

We can use Freire's ideas to frame youth library services as conscious social activism aimed at countering misinformation. In his book *Pedagogy of the Oppressed* (2018), Freire countered prevailing "banking" models of education, which conceived of students as empty banks into which teachers deposit knowledge in the form of objective fact divorced from sociopolitical context. In Freire's view, the goal of education should be to address social issues such as inequity, violence, racism, and poverty, teaching content within the sociopolitical reality in which it exists. This socially conscious education model requires guiding students to understand the world beyond the classroom, including the study of contemporary sociopolitical controversies, such as the ethics of abortion and the rights of LGBTQ+ people.

We suggest applying Freire's focus on socially conscious action to youth library services, reframing our view of librarianship from politically neutral information services to active sociopolitical engagement. Young people cannot learn to recognize and critique misinformation unless they understand the broken social structures from which it stems, and we cannot guide them to examine these structures without inserting ourselves into the political discourse.

This is particularly important in the case of library services for youth from oppressed groups, such as Black, Indigenous, People of Color (BIPOC), and LGBTQ+ youth—groups deprived of equitable social power and privilege by the more privileged groups that oppress them. The concept of oppression lies at the center of Freire's work. He suggests that education offers a path for oppressed groups to become empowered. Without equitable educational opportunities, he argues, members of oppressed groups are unable to recognize and reflect on the unfairness of their situations and to devise paths toward freedom from oppression. This leads us to question the North American conceptions of individual freedoms, freedom of expression, and economic freedom: These freedoms are guaranteed for whom?

As librarians and library scholars, we can teach young people to become critical of the information they encounter online as well as the information that is missing from public discourses to enable them to become more reflective of their own positions in society and more empowered to resist oppression. It's also important to recall that in Freire's perspective, education is a dialogic act in which the teacher and student both teach and learn with each other. Freire asserts that any discussion of social oppression must be undertaken with those who are oppressed. He sees education as a revolutionary way of addressing the social conditions of the underprivileged, oriented toward freedom in the sense of empowering the disempowered to become free from oppression. As educated librarians and therefore, members of at least one privileged social group, we must work with youth belonging to oppressed groups to understand their lived realities and to privilege their experiences and perspectives.

Freire's pedagogy also defends the school as a space that should privilege the open discussion of ideas, even if they are controversial; effective education requires learning about the societies in which we live. By extension, libraries as educational organizations must privilege the open discussion of ideas to teach young people how to identify and challenge misinformation. We must combine teaching information literacy and critical thinking skills with studying social issues and controversies, rather than focusing on "information" in itself as "correct" or "incorrect." Youth cannot form their own opinions about abortion, for example, if they don't have the opportunity to study all sides of the relevant arguments, and they are less likely to recognize abortion misinformation if they don't understand why it's a controversial issue.

At its core, Freire's work teaches us that education (and library) services are not neutral actions but instead tools for social change. Fidelis and Gomes (2022) build on his ideas to argue that information can be used for public good (in the form of social emancipation) or for public harm (in the form of ideological indoctrination) and stress the importance of conscious information mediation as a process of ongoing reflection of the impact of library services on the societies in which they exist. Rather than shying away from partisan and controversial topics, youth librarians must take upon themselves the responsibility of serving as integrated members of society who bear responsibility for active social education for the public good. Youth librarians can use intentional, reflective dialogue with young people to promote understanding among disparate groups while making conscious efforts to preserve and center the cultural knowledge of oppressed social groups.

CONCLUSION: SOCIALLY CONSCIOUS YOUTH SERVICES IN A MISINFORMATION SOCIETY

This discussion highlights the urgency of framing youth librarianship as education for the public good and teaches us that librarianship in itself is a political act. It is up to youth librarians to teach young people how to identify and challenge the social contexts that give rise to misleading and false discourse. The US and Brazilian political insurrections as well as the Brazilian ESP movement discussed above point to the potential harms of a misinformation society left unchecked. We know that merely refuting false information rarely convinces those who believe it and can, in fact, lead to reinforcing it, especially when belief is tied to ideology (Simão, 2019). Much more effective than outright refutation is teaching alternate narratives that employ critical information literacy skills, such as teaching young people how propagandists create and distribute disinformation campaigns. Once young people learn how disinformation is created, they are much less likely to fall prey to it.

A common LIS response to the misinformation society is the suggestion that librarians can "solve" the problem of misinformation by teaching young people how to identify "good" or "trustworthy" information, often with a checklist or list of questions to apply when looking at information. This is a mechanical and limited way of acting with subjects who are socially dynamic. Providing simple evaluation tools without engaging in shared reflective discussion removes the librarian from the information ecosystem, leaving young people to interpret for themselves the messages they encounter in the media. It also puts the responsibility for controlling the spread of misinformation on the message receivers, rather than the senders. Instead, we must play an active role as educational partners with youth, engaging together in critical examinations of the social systems that give rise to misinformation narratives; teaching with examples from daily life; and more specifically, situations that are part of young people's daily lived experience. This action engages young people in useful discussions with an emphasis on understanding how misinformation systems perpetuate the oppression of groups many of them belong to, such as BIPOC, LGBTQ+, women, the poor, and others. It's a tall order, to be sure, but it offers librarianship a positive path for combating the misinformation society and for helping to build a more positive future information ecosystem for the world's youth.

DISCUSSION QUESTIONS

- What social forces contribute to the rise and perpetuation of misinformation in the current information society?
- What are some potential social harms of a misinformation society? Can you identify specific cases?
- Examine the debate around LIS as a politically neutral profession and its implications for addressing misinformation. Do you think librarians should adopt a neutral stance?
- How can youth services create an open and inclusive space for discussions on controversial topics while promoting critical information literacy skills and conscious information mediation?
- What are some potential issues that could arise in trying to teach information literacy skills? What can be done to address these issues?

REFERENCES

Agosto, D. E. (2018). *Information literacy and libraries in the age of fake news.* Santa Barbara, CA: Libraries Unlimited.

Agosto, D. E., & Oltmann, S. M. (2022). Guest editorial: The complexity of teaching and learning about mis- and disinformation. *Information and Learning Sciences, 122*(1/2). https://doi.org/10.1108/ILS-01-2022-263.

Araújo, C. A. Ávila. (2021). Pós-verdade: novo objeto de estudo para a ciência da informação. *Informação & Informação, 26*(1), 94–111.

Braga, R. (2023, January 11). The insurrection in Brazil is part of a broader crisis of trust. *Time.* https://time.com/6246475/brazil-insurrection-bolsonaro-disinformation/.

Ferreira, J. M. de G., & Souza, G. P. de. (2018). Reflexões acerca do movimento 'Escola sem Partido' inspiradas pelas teorias de Paulo Freire e Pierre Bourdieu. *Revista Educação E Emancipação, 11*(2), 34–59. https://doi.org/10.18764/2358-4319.v11n2p34-59.

Fidelis, M. B., & Gomes, H. F. (2022). Mediação da informação e ação comunicativa Habermasiana. *Logeion: Filosofia Da Informação, 9*(1), 91–111.

Freire, P. (2018). *Pedagogy of the oppressed* (50th anniversary ed.). Bloomsbury.

Keyes, R. (2004). *The post-truth era: Dishonesty and deception in contemporary life.* St. Martin's Press.

Simão, R. B. (2019). Firehosing: por que fatos não vão chegar aos bolsonaristas. *Le Monde Diplomatique Brasil, 137*, 14.

The Economist. (2019, March 14). *Jair Bolsonaro, Brazil's president, is a master of social media.* https://www.economist.com/the-americas/2019/03/14/jair-bolsonaro-brazils -president-is-a-master-of-social-media.

13

A Rainbow of Diverse Opportunities

SERVING LGBTQIA+ TEENS IN SCHOOL AND PUBLIC LIBRARIES

Jamie Campbell Naidoo and Gwendolyn Nixon

Over the years, the role of libraries has evolved from a place where patrons only check out books or search for information to a third space where patrons attend events, collaborate on projects, and build community. This role of a third space can be especially important for the lesbian, gay, bisexual, transgender, queer/questioning, intersex, asexual, and expansive (LGBTQIA+) young adult, who may be navigating self-esteem issues and family struggles related to their identity while dealing with normal teenage challenges. The opportunity for librarians to provide a safe haven for LGBTQIA+ teens is important now more than ever, particularly in a world filled with anti-LGBTQIA+ rhetoric and government-sanctioned censorship of queer books. This chapter offers suggestions librarians can use to jump-start this work by providing inclusive spaces, reflective materials, engaging programs, and supportive staff.

SAFE SPACES

School and public libraries serving teens can function as a third, safe space for young adults, where they can socialize and also provide a safe place for LGBTQIA+, who, research suggests are much more vulnerable than other teens. Librarians can denote these spaces as "safe" through the use of specialized signage explicitly identifying the library as an inclusive space for queer youth or via buttons with pronouns or various pride symbols to show their support of LGBTQIA+ teens. Gender-neutral bathrooms are also an easy way to signal to nonbinary youth that the library is a welcoming place. Safe spaces should create an inclusive atmosphere that allows LGBTQIA+ teens to feel welcome to express themselves and socialize with peers. Library posters with a broad representation of diverse individuals, including LGBTQIA+ celebrities, authors, and athletes, can provide role models for queer youth or simply an opportunity to see their lives reflected.

LGBTQIA+ teens, particularly, require confidentiality in patron records and discretion when they require help locating materials. Libraries serving these teenagers are encouraged to have the option of self-checkout or at the very least, a robust e-book collection for those teens who do not want to be observed checking out LGBTQIA+ materials.

Curated book displays can also provide opportunities for LGBTQIA+ teens and their cisgender and heterosexual peers to learn about the contributions of LGBTQIA+ individuals and enjoy titles featuring queer characters. Something librarians should be mindful of, however, is that while a pride display can be welcoming to some LGBTQIA+ teens, it can also be threatening to closeted queer youth. An alternative is an inclusive display where titles are integrated naturally by non-LGBTQIA+ topic, such as As Seen on BookTok, graphic novels, book to movie, survival stories, or thrillers. Staff and/or peer recommendations can discreetly mention the presence of LGBTQIA+ characters within the text of their posted review without obviously outing the patron selecting the book.

Another way for librarians to create a safe space for queer teens is by establishing themselves as allies of LGBTQIA+ youth. They can advocate for queer youth at the administrative level and establish themselves as a resource for those wanting to learn about the local queer community and to support queer teens. A useful resource, which can be adapted for librarian use, is the Northwest Network of Bisexual, Trans, Lesbian and Gay Survivors of Abuse's (2001) "Quick Organizational Audit: LGBT Visibility and Inclusion." This resource provides practical suggestions for conducting a walk-through audit of a physical space.

COLLECTION DEVELOPMENT

All youth libraries should have developmentally appropriate, high-quality print and digital materials that normalize the experiences of LGBTQIA+ individuals and provide an opportunity for queer teens to feel accepted and validated. A diverse, intersectional collection is essential for LGBTQIA+ teens to see themselves in the materials they encounter, for their self-worth, and to encourage them to use the library.

Any library interested in attracting hard-to-reach young adults must keep their collection updated and relevant. When purchasing new titles or evaluating existing ones, it is important for library staff to understand changes in terminology and recent societal views in order to effectively address LGBTQIA+ characters and themes. Titles should be reviewed for content, for example, how a character reacts when they learn that an important person in their life is LGBTQIA+, or how individuals handle their LGBTQIA+ identity. Titles should also be free of stereotypes or outdated language. The simple presence of queer characters does not equal positive or accurate portrayals. A wide array of topics should be covered in library materials to meet the diverse needs of contemporary LGBTQIA+ teens from a variety of cultural backgrounds. Collections should include subcultures of the queer community and represent intersectionality of race, ethnicity, gender identity and expression, age, ability, religious affiliation, and diverse socioeconomic status.

Another critical consideration when selecting LGBTQIA+ materials is whether they meet the standards of the library's collection development policy. Ensuring all titles adhere to a school district's or library's policy for purchasing protects the librarian when censorship challenges arise. It is imperative that librarians be well versed in their library process for book challenges. When defending LGBTQIA+ materials, an updated collection development policy is essential as well as an updated reconsideration policy. Talk to your library colleagues and administration ahead of time so there are no surprises, and communicate with your library board or school board as appropriate. Seeking support from state and national library groups, including the American Library Association Office for Intellectual Freedom, is key when faced with challenges of queer youth materials. Librarians should remember that their goal is to provide a library that is welcoming to all users, especially vulnerable groups such as LGBTQIA+ teens.

While building a balanced library collection is critical, a balanced library collection of LGBTQIA+ materials does not mean that it should include antiqueer materials. If a librarian is pressured by their local government or administration to purchase anti-LGBTQIA+ content, the materials should equally meet the library's collection development policy, be respectful of the target audience's understanding, and not promote propaganda or hate speech. Currently, no anti-queer youth books meet these criteria.

The display and physical shelving of the library's LGBTQIA+ print titles are another important aspect to consider when serving queer teens. Some librarians may choose to use a unique genre label (often a rainbow flag) on the spine of their books in order for teen readers to easily identify queer characters in books. Having a display of queer titles sends the message to patrons that your library is an inclusive space with titles for all different kinds of people. A disadvantage of this method is that separate displays or labels open these titles up to challenges from the public or out teens reading an LGBTQIA+ book when this is something that may make them uncomfortable. No one method for organizing collections works for all youth libraries. Rather, librarians should do what feels best for their community or ask teens for feedback on displays and collection genrefication.

Whatever is the best fit for your library, queer authors and books with LGBTQIA+ characters should be readily findable via the online search catalog using appropriate subject headings. Teen patrons should have the ability to easily locate LGBTQIA+ materials within the library without assistance. Consistent and current terminology should be used in MARC records, subject headings, and tags. If a library catalog uses outdated terminology, edit subject headings using controlled vocabulary from trusted sources such as Homosaurus (https://homosaurus.org/), which strives to have a common, universal search language for LGBTQIA+ materials. Youth librarians can also post online lists of recommended LGBTQIA+ teen books via curated lists on the library's website.

Online collections and digital book lists can also be developed so users can easily click through the recommended titles from the privacy of their own device. A rich collection of e-books and e-audiobooks of LGBTQIA+ titles should be included so teens can access these books without having to physically check out a title and bring it into a home that may be discouraging of their identity.

Librarian allies seeking to be proactive about the representation of LGBTQIA+ characters in their library can perform an LGBTQIA+ diversity audit of their collection, which will provide a snapshot of collection representation and help librarians determine gaps in their collection (Naidoo, 2023). Titles can be analyzed to determine LGBTQIA+ representation in primary and secondary characters, themes, and topics. This information is usually organized in a spreadsheet with separate columns to capture specific facts of representation that are to be analyzed. Examining the LGBTQIA+ identity of, for example, authors, illustrators, actors, and audiobook narrators, is also important, but librarians should additionally consider if queer creators are creating non-LGBTQIA+ materials. If so, this can be tabulated separately to differentiate between materials with queer content versus materials without queer content but by LGBTQIA+ creators. Ideally, the library's collection will have both types of materials.

PROGRAMMING

Effective, engaging programming is vital to creating a place where every teen feels welcome. One simple way to have programming that is LGBTQIA+ friendly is to ensure that all programs offered by the library are safe for all attendees, regardless of identity. Queer-centric clubs and programs send a clear message that the library is welcoming and inclusive of LGBTQIA+ patrons. However, queer teens may have different levels of being "out"—to themselves, their families, or friends. Like any population, there is no one-size-fits-all description. It is important to include the target audience in the planning process when creating a programming plan for queer youth. School librarians can contact their school's Sexuality and Gender Alliance or other LGBTQIA+ clubs for guidance, and public/school librarians can contact local LGBTQIA+ youth organizations for recommendations. An LGBTQIA+ library advisory committee of community members can also help assist in the development of queer programs to ensure relevancy and sensitivity, provide cultural training and workshops for librarians, and support library staff faced with anti-queer sentiment and challenges.

Libraries hoping to draw in teens should have a robust volunteer program. Even the busiest teenager likely has to complete service hours for graduation and will be looking for a welcoming space to volunteer. Public librarians can partner with school librarians to host evening study hours, movie nights, comic-cons, and alternative proms either specifically for or inclusive of LGBTQIA+ teens. School and public libraries can also host LGBTQIA+ family events. These can be targeted to LGBTQIA+ teens and their families or involve all members of the community but ensure that the event is inclusive, safe, and welcoming to queer teens.

The library or an entire school community may celebrate Pride weeks or months. This is a great time to showcase the library's LGBTQIA+ titles and re-sources. Teen volunteers can take ownership of the month and plan programs, create attractive displays, and make eye-catching bulletin boards in celebration. Created by the InsideOUT (n.d.) charity in New Zealand, the Out on the Shelves resource provides recommended booklists, an online zine for youth, and dynamic display suggestions for librarians on how to create welcoming displays for queer youth.

STAFFING

Youth services librarians should also have a working familiarity with LGBTQIA+ terminology. A useful source for adults is provided by the Welcoming Schools Definitions to Help Understand Gender and Sexual Orientation (Human Rights Campaign Foundation Welcoming Schools, 2020). Never presume to know how a patron would like to be addressed. Instead of saying, "she would like to borrow this book," use "this patron" or "this student." Some school districts and public libraries have the option for "Name Goes By" in their official records. If you have this option, be sure to check the field before you address an LGBTQIA+ patron by a name they no longer use.

Regular professional development on serving LGBTQIA+ patrons of all ages is recommended. Youth services staff should be trained on how to promote and ensure a safe space for teen participants. Librarians should be prepared to intervene immediately if there is language or behavior from young people or library colleagues that goes against the rules of the safe space. It is rec-ommended that signage be posted throughout the library with guidelines for appropriate language, with a zero tolerance policy for hate speech.

CONCLUSION

School and public librarians are in the unique position to make a difference in the lives of their teen LGBTQIA+ patrons, which is especially important in light of current anti-LGBTQIA+, particularly anti-trans, rhetoric and rampant bans of queer books. Youth librarians can provide a safe haven for queer teens, using the suggestions in this chapter to inspire and guide their work. Numerous other resources are also available to assist librarians as they engage with LGBTQIA+ youth. DiScala et al. (2020) provide an organic list of recommended resources with other ideas for school librarians, and Naidoo (2021) suggests book awards and various online resources for all librarians serving queer youth. Armed with these tools, youth librarians indeed have a rainbow of diverse opportunities for serving the informational and recreational needs of queer youth in school and public libraries.

DISCUSSION QUESTIONS

- What are the defining features of a "safe space" in libraries for young adults?
- Should librarians be responsible if something dangerous or hazardous occurs in a library's public space?
- How can non-youth adult library staff better ensure equitable library services to LGBTQIA+ youth?

REFERENCES

DiScala, J., Gay-Milliken, L., & Trzieciakewicz, S. (2020). *Annotated bibliography of LGBTQ resources for school librarians*. http://bit.ly/LGBTQforKQ.

Human Rights Campaign Foundation Welcoming Schools. (2020). *Definitions to help understand gender and sexual orientation*. https://assets2.hrc.org/welcoming-schools/documents/WS_Gender_Sexual_Orientation_Definitions_Adults.pdf.

InsideOUT. (n.d.). *Out on the shelves*. https://outontheshelves.insideout.org.nz/.

Naidoo, J. C. (2021). *Inclusive services & programs: Welcoming LGBTQ+ youth & their families to your library*. https://tinyurl.com/welcomeLGBTQyouth.

Naidoo, J. C. (2023). *LGBTQIA+ diversity audit for library collections*. https://tinyurl.com/lgbtqdiversityaudit.

Northwest Network of Bisexual, Trans, Lesbian and Gay Survivors of Abuse. (2001). *Quick organizational audit: LGBT visibility and inclusion*. https://vawnet.org/material/quick-organizational-audit-lgbt-visibility-and-inclusion.

14

The Challenge of Being Expert in Youth Literature

Mary Ann Harlan

Youth services librarians frequently find their way to librarianship because of their self-identity as readers and their love of books. The intention is to share this love with young people so that they, too, will come to love reading as we do. The assumptions in these statements need to be unpacked. The first assumes that librarians are librarians because they love reading. While this is not always the case, my experience as a librarian and as a library educator provides plenty of anecdotal evidence for the truth of this assumption, from introductions in my courses to noting popular conference sessions over 20-plus years. However, anecdote is supported by research that indicates library and information science (LIS) education perpetuates this assumption by catering to this belief. As Barriage et al. (2021) discuss, syllabi in LIS youth services courses have an "inordinate focus on becoming familiar with literature for children and youth" (p. 1).

Professional organizations further this focus through awards and recommended book lists. This has a de facto result of positioning librarians as experts in the field of youth literature. The concept of the role of youth librarianship as developing expertise in youth literature is a cyclical process—students come to LIS careers because of their own experiences with libraries as collections of books, LIS education perpetuates the emphasis on reading and books, and then graduates put into practice the elements of reading promotion and their love of books. While services exist beyond this in libraries and have for a long time, the field of youth services in LIS still focuses on libraries within a traditional role of a collection of books that we promote.

The second assumption, and one I wish to challenge for prospective youth services librarians, is that our identity as readers makes us experts on books, and perhaps reading. This inordinate focus on familiarity ignores

1. how we read analytically and
2. how we read affectively.

The assumption ignores how our identities affect both of those components of textual engagement. It also ignores the fact that we do not undertake our own reading with a theoretical lens. Without unpacking both analytical and affective reading for the individual reader, we leave open the question, can one be an expert in youth literature just because they read youth literature? The challenge for youth services librarians is to engage analytically with both the text and their own assumptions about youth as readers rather than assuming expertise.

While library education pays more attention to the cognitive process of reading, it does not particularly engaging in the so-called reading wars relating to our understanding of the cognitive process of reading development with much depth. How we learn to read is hotly debated in reading education—the use of context clues in decoding, development of phonics through repetition, and reading skills, such as summarizing and prediction, are just a few elements of reading instruction that are subject to debate. Every few years, reading educators are treated to new theories suggesting the most effective ways to teach reading. Usually, librarians find themselves searching for their place in these debates and relying on their role as resource providers. For adolescent readers, librarians find themselves identifying resources that are of high interest with low reading levels, or finding books on a Lexile or AR level for a parent demanding their child have a book at that level (typically, not an easy ask and one that ignores how reading levels are determined). In these instances, the mere familiarity of resources is not enough to engage this question thoroughly. Librarians must understand the underlying theories of the debate, if they are to suggest a certain level of reading expertise.

Nevertheless, that is not particularly what I am worried about in challenging the notion of expertise in "books," which is different from being experts in the process of reading. I put books in quotes because the field positions itself as one with a predominance of experts in reading, particularly in fiction. Not that nonfiction is immune to this notion of expertise in books. However, the discipline primarily focuses on the potential role of fiction in the lives of teens. The core question here is, does reading a lot make one an expert in books? Assuming this expertise is significant because librarians gatekeep youth literature—along with publishers and teachers. Librarians review books, purchase them for their patrons, and promote them. In doing so we have an impact on what books are available and what trends guide the market. Often, we do this without asking ourselves what makes us experts? How are we reading? How does our self-identity as readers inform our positioning?

Let's begin with the question, are we reading analytically? There is an academic discipline dedicated to reading analytically, literary criticism. Literary criticism requires close reading and an analytical lens. Close reading engages a text through theory, and there are different theoretical lenses that one can apply. For example, we can use critical race theory, because it has been adapted for literary criticism, feminism, Marxism, queer theory, or poststructuralism. Each of these approaches will yield a different reading experience. And, it takes time and practice to master the close reading and application of theory. Lest we think young adult literature is of value only to the reader, there is a growing and robust community of researchers that is engaged in literary criticism of young adult literature, which should be attended to in the exploration of reading analytically.

Angie Thomas's case study, *The Hate U Give*, illustrates the point that reading analytically may produce a different reading experience and textual information. *The Hate U Give* (2017) is the story of a teenage girl (Starr) experiencing the police shooting of her friend. The book debuted at number one on the New York Times Young Adult Hardcover Bestsellers list, spent 50 weeks on the list (as of April 2023, it has been on the list for 249 weeks), received positive reviews not just in trade journals but also in the mainstream adult press, was made into a movie, and won the Printz honor from the Young Adult Library Services. It is a core text in youth collections and on dozens of recommended reading lists. However, close readings by literature scholars have suggested different reading experiences of this text that are more nuanced than the accolades suggest. For instance, Kaylee Jangula Mootz (2020) in critiquing police violence young adult as a genre asks, "Who are these books really for?" She argues that while books such as *The Hate U Give* are road maps for young activists to find their voice, there is also a concern that "texts about Black youth activism often seem to be roadmaps for understanding whiteness during times of racial tension" (p. 64) and for providing an empathetic learning experience for white readers. Other scholars have suggested the same—that it can be a road map for youth activism for non-Black readers (Sharma, 2018) rather than a book written for Black youth.

Another analysis explored Starr's code-switching as a metaphor for a national (non)identity among marginalized people (Shelat, 2019). This can be seen as a counter-narrative to Mootz (2020), or at the very least, an expansion of her roadmap to activism argument. These all suggest that there are other ways to read *The Hate U Give* rather than as a universal experience of Black youth or a story they "need" for representation. Each analysis requires a close read through a theoretical lens rather than a broad awareness that the book exists and is well reviewed. Reading for awareness, for review, for collection development, and/or for readers' advisory does not necessarily mean reading analytically.

If we are to distance ourselves from literary criticism, considering it outside the scope of LIS and only tangentially related to how we define our expertise in youth literature, we can then, and should, engage a different theory of reading and how we read to develop so-called expertise. Louise Rosenblatt's (1982) reader response theory might best describe how we engage in the experience of reading and how we presume others encounter the process. Librarians reviewing texts for purchase, promotion, or for bibliotherapy is a practice rooted in reader response theory. Rosenblatt (1982) defines reading as "a transaction, a two-way process, involving a reader and a text at a particular time under particular circumstances" (p. 268). Rosenblatt points out that readers make choices when faced with a text, a mental stance toward the text whether they are reading for efferent (or informational) reasons or aesthetic reasons. And so, as librarians, when we sit down to read, we also make choices—are we reading for self, or are we reading for an imagined youth reader? And can we consider ourselves experts in the imagined youth reader?

The concept of the imagined reader undergirds how we build collections—who are we purchasing these books for? Who are we promoting these books to? Any imagined reader is going to be rooted in our own biases and viewed through the lens of adult memories of youth. If we do not unpack how we view youth and our bias, we risk flattening the imagined reader. We read the book as the primary reader either as our current adult self or our remembered teen self. When we read aesthetically, the primary question is, did we like it? This does not develop expertise in the texts. It provides awareness of the text; we know the plot, the characters, and likely the major themes. We are reading to decide whether to purchase and how to promote the text to a specific audience. This demands that we interrogate our imagined reader.

I wish to return to *The Hate U Give*. While mentoring a teacher on a research project that disrupts common beliefs about *The Adventures of Huckleberry Finn* as an antiracist novel, we spent a great deal of time discussing Bishop's (1990) metaphor of reading as windows, mirrors, and sliding glass doors. I was researching fiction as an information source for identity development, while she was investigating how to encourage a critical read of Huckleberry Finn. We were finding that her students, who were primarily white, had difficulty dismissing the common belief that the novel was a treatise against slavery, even though they were able to engage in serious criticism of the treatment of Jim, and the ending in particular. I was finding the same students engaged in independent reading by looking for the mirrors Bishop spoke of, even when the text may have been far from their own experience, creating a fun-house mirror understanding of the text.

While there were multiple instances of the fun-house mirror effect, with and without guided reading, the one involving *The Hate U Give* stood out in

Mary Ann Harlan

terms of my imagined reader and the nature of texts labeled diverse (which subtly others the text from white experience and is problematic in and of itself). After "binge reading the f--- out" of the book, one white girl discussed how she related to Starr. In comparing Starr's experience, attending a private, primarily white school while living in a Black neighborhood and the code-switching with which she struggled, the teen in question noted that it was the same as her own "mask wearing" as she navigated different friendship groups. Her community was also not immune to police violence against Black people or other people of color. At the time, they were dealing with racialized violence, after a young Black man died from a knife injury, because the local police department prevented the paramedics from responding. Still, this student primarily related to Starr through a personalized story about friendship without recognition of the racial elements of her code-switching. Binging may have had an impact because it was hardly a close read, but when a book speaks to a reader, binging often happens. This was not how my imagined reader (white, female in this case) would have experienced the text. Rather, I was expecting the reader to experience the text as a window into an unfamiliar world, fostering empathy for Starr's life as a Black girl in America.

The challenge the field faces is that an overemphasis on reading widely does not make us experts in young adult texts or in literacy. Without unpacking the assumptions of our own reading identity, adult perspectives on youth, and the media created (by adults) for them, we risk perpetuating media and practices that fail the youth we serve as well as the youth we wish to serve. Assuming expertise because we read widely without acknowledging the imagined reader, as well as the unexpected reader, is just that, an assumption that does not hold up in terms of either texts or readers. We should be addressing our assumptions regarding the imagined reader before claiming expertise. Youth are, like all identities, not a monolith. There are intersecting identities and differing experiences that affect their reading experience and what they might bring to a text. Therefore, how we read as librarians is a political act. Our imagined reader is a pawn in the politics of the discipline, and youth literature is merely a vehicle for adults defining youth identity.

For instance, adolescent developmental theory, while prevalent in the field, is only one theory of youth lived experience. The idea that adolescence is a time of strum und drang (storm and stress) has been critiqued quite thoroughly, and those critiques need to be engaged. Critical youth theory not only critiques developmentalism and biological determinism; it suggests that youth is a culturally, socially, and historically produced construct. It posits a variety of ways of understanding not only the creation of the category of adolescence but also the lived experience of youth. These are only two approaches to understanding adolescents as imagined readers. Is the lens through which you read a young adult book one of biological determinism? Do adolescents develop in stages? Does that mean all works need to focus on risk-taking and identity development with plenty of dramatic conflict? On the other hand, if we consider youth as a term and age constructed to serve adult needs (work, policy, etc.), how does this change the imagined reader? Do we then engage Trites's (1998) argument that youth literature is about power and repression? Perhaps we understand youth as an intersectional identity; what might that mean in relation to how we read?

I recently asked a friend, is the media reflecting youth, or are youth reflecting media? The question is rhetorical. Perry Nodelman (2016), wrote:

> The adults who write, publish, and purchase books for young people do so because they perceive young people as needing a special literature they cannot produce themselves; accordingly, the texts these adults produce represent adult voices speaking to and for young people. (p. 267)

Adults come to a text with their own lens. When reading young adult literature, they read through the memory of their youth rather than being in the moment of youth. This memory, which can be faulty, may manifest as a reading of a text that represents our memory of our youth rather than a representation of youth in a current moment. Examining how we remember ourselves as teens is necessary to recognize how we read a text. And we should consciously name the theory of youth we are using as a lens. We do not leave behind our theoretical beliefs or lived experiences when we encounter the first page. Our own world beliefs will underlie how we read a text, which may affect how we understand representation within any given text, much like the young woman above, who read *The Hate U Give*. We cannot claim expertise in the text as a text for young adults without this acknowledgment and examination.

If we focus on knowing ourselves and how this affects how we imagine a reader, we may serve youth more fully. We need to understand what we bring to a text when we are reading to evaluate, review, promote, or advise individual readers. We also need to develop a relationship with youth. We cannot adequately establish a text as a young adult text without young adults. Yes, it is a publisher's designation, and the books within the category share similar traits. But it is the reader that determines how it might be representative. We need to admit that adult control over a text at various levels, such as authoring, publishing, and promoting, may other the intended/imagined reader through flaws in memory, unacknowledged bias, or plain old "I am an adult and therefore, know better" attitudes.

As we read, we need to engage with other disciplines. Collaboration presents an interesting opportunity in terms of developing expertise. The field has some opportunities in addressing the challenge. The first, and perhaps easiest, is to acknowledge that we are not experts in literature per se, but that we are knowledgeable about what is published. It may be semantics, but it does not presume to understand how a book will be read. This is particularly important in disrupting how a text might serve as bibliotherapy, fulfill a common request, or contribute to empathy building. It doesn't extend the librarian's role into that of a social worker or therapist; instead, it recognizes their role in readers' advisory. It also frames how we review and award excellence through our organizations, suggesting a need for collaboration with other organizations or people who have expertise in craft or analysis.

Rather than studying what is published or a youth canon, we can and should study theories of youth, particularly those beyond developmentalism. Bernier (2019) has made this point regarding LIS youth services curriculum quite strongly, but as soon-to-be or current practitioners, who define the field, it is also your responsibility to continue examining critically your own positioning, beliefs, and practices within the discipline and your service. We should emphasize practices that center on youth defining themselves. This should go beyond reading, but when we engage in understanding youth needs through advisory boards, etc., we should do so by allowing them to define themselves as readers, as the gatekeepers for youth literature, and as authors of their own experiences. The TL;DR (too long; didn't read) here is that reading widely does not make us experts; it makes us readers, and those are not reciprocal identities.

DISCUSSION QUESTIONS

- What does Harlan's concern for a lack of librarian self-awareness have in common with Petrella's essay (chapter 23) on whiteness?
- How does Harlan's critique of "youth development" comport with Rhodenizer's (chapter 21) profile of the Lubuto Library Partners?
- How would you characterize the value of your own level of "expertise" on young adult literature for young adult users?

REFERENCES

Barriage, S., DiGiacomo, D., & Greenhalgh, S. (2021). thinking beyond library and information science: Interdisciplinary inspiration for children and youth services curricula. *Journal of Education for Library and Information Science, 63*(1), 1–18.

Bernier, A. (2019, April). Isn't it time for youth services instruction to grow up? Superstition or scholarship. *Journal of Education for Library and Information Science 60*(2), 118–38.

Bishop, R. S. (1990, March). Windows and mirrors: Children's books and parallel cultures. In *California State University reading conference: 14th annual conference proceedings* (pp. 3–12).

Mootz, K. J. (2020). Who are these books really for? Police-violence YA, Black youth activism, and the implied White audience. In R. Fitzsimmons & C. A. Wilson (Eds.), *Beyond the blockbusters: Themes and trends in contemporary young adult fiction* (pp. 63–79). University Press of Mississippi.

Nodelman, P. (2016). The hidden child in the hidden adult. *Jeunesse: Young People, Texts, Cultures, 8*(1), 266–77. https://doi.org/10.3138/jeunesse.8.1.266.

Rosenblatt, L. M. (1982). The literary transaction: Evocation and response. *Theory into Practice, 21*(4), 268–77. https://doi.org/10.1080/00405848209543018.

Sharma, M. D. (2018). *Agency for the child in* Esperanza Rising *and* The Hate U Give*: A call to young non-Black readers.* ProQuest Dissertations Publishing.

Shelat, J. (2019). "I swear those things are so fresh": Sneakers, race, and mobility in *The Hate U Give. CEA Critic, 81*(1), 70–74. https://doi.org/10.1353/cea.2019.0011.

Trites, R. S. (1998). *Disturbing the universe: Power and repression in adolescent literature.* University of Iowa Press.

15

The New Teenager Presents New Challenges to Libraries

Mike A. Males

The disappearance of the traditional "teenager" over the last generation represents one of America's most abrupt and startling social revolutions, so cataclysmic in its implications that major institutions abjectly refuse to acknowledge it. While libraries have resisted popular repressions in the past, especially censorship, the challenge in confronting today's repressive institutional maladaptation to a dynamic, diverse new generation is unprecedented.

Combining social science and popular theories, the traditional "teenager" (originally coined as a 1940s corporate marketing target) is characterized by innate impulsiveness and heightened response to short-term reward, promoting rash behaviors such as excessive crime, violence, sexual irresponsibility, alienation/rebellion, and risk-taking (Strang et al., 2013). The rigid popular narrative blames "teenagers" for gun violence, drug overdose, suicide, educational failure, and a mental health "crisis" driven by peer culture.

This chapter uses California's more reliable, long-term statistics representing the leading edge of national trends to argue that the traditional high-risk "teenager" (both juvenile and young adult ages) no longer exists. This revolution has profound implications that American institutions, including libraries, not only are failing to avail but are also meeting with confusion, fear, and hostility that threaten the young and national order alike.

THE VANISHING "TEENAGER"

The statistical documentation of the disappearance of the traditional "teen-ager" is compelling. Demographically, from 1995 to 2022, California's popula-tion ages 10 to 19 grew by 800,000 and became 72 percent of color (Hispanic, Asian, Black, Native, mixed race, and other nonwhite) (US Census Bureau, 2023). Panicked "experts" predicted these trends would spawn violent adoles-cent "super-predators," alienates, and epidemic social crises.

In fact, from 1995 through 2022, rates of total crimes among Californians ages 10 to 19 plummeted by 89 percent, including a 78 percent decline in vio-lence and a 96 percent plunge in property offenses (California Department of Justice [CDOJ], 2023). Crimes thought singularly "teenage," such as robbery (down 81 percent), arson (down 94 percent), vandalism (down 94 percent), and petty theft/shoplifting (down 97 percent) are disappearing among Califor-nia teens. Meanwhile, teens' rates of gun fatality fell by 75 percent, homicides also fell 75 percent, births by mothers younger than 20 fell 85 percent (Centers for Disease Control and Prevention [CDC], 2023), high school dropout rates declined 63 percent, and college enrollment (up 34 percent) and degree rates (up 94 percent) increased despite higher tuitions (US Census Bureau, 2023). The 131,000 K–12 schools, despite suffering mass shootings like elsewhere, remain among America's safest places from gun violence, with fatal shooting levels among its 50 million students and 5 million adults far below those of homes or public areas and on par with numbers seen in Germany's (Males, 2023a). During this time frame, most troubles once thought to characterize teenagers reached their lowest levels ever reliably recorded.

That these solid, standard-referenced statistics appear shocking only demonstrates the degree to which American authorities and interests are refusing to rationally evaluate trends in issues facing teenagers. Other than California's decriminalization of marijuana, which modestly reduced arrests among all ages, laws and policies do not account for these improvements. In fact, policy interventions in teenage lives have proven useless or harmful. Ar-rests of youths for "status offenses," such as curfew, truancy, "incorrigibility," and youth-control measures nosedived from a peak of 230,000 in 1969 to just 1,200 in 2021. Youths referred to juvenile probation have fallen from 200,000 per year in the mid-1990s to just 16,000 in 2022 (CDOJ, 2023), while incarcer-ations of California juveniles in state and local facilities fell from over 20,000 to around 2,600 in 2023. Never have more California teenagers been on the streets than today.

Rather, the massive reductions in crime, violence, births, and dropout among teenagers and young adults stem from fewer grade-schoolers and younger teens entering justice and treatment systems in the first place. Reduc-tions in poverty and toxic lead exposure appear to have major beneficial effects

Mike A. Males

(Nevin, 2021; Thomson and Ryberg, 2021), but younger people themselves deserve credit. By traditional definitions and broad standard measures, today's adolescents and young adults no longer are the feared demographic formerly known as "teenagers." The criminal arrest rates for California teenagers—whose trends are harbingers of national trends—have fallen below those of middle-agers in their 40s and 50s. Both juvenile and adult teens no longer are "at-risk" or "crime-prone" populations.

These developments present new concepts previously unheard of in social science, overturning decades of faulty theories about "adolescent development" and "brain science." Unfortunately, institutional America, discombobulated by the new teenager, remains trapped in its "always bad and getting worse" narrative, disparaging young people with rampant falsifications. Major media headlines reporting ever-more trivial incidents, such as school or amusement park fistfights, exemplify this trend.

The problem stems from biased perceptions and prejudice. When evaluating potential threats, the rule 25 years ago and earlier was that statistically, teenagers were more likely to commit violent, property, vandalism, and drug offenses than were older adults. In 1980, six times more Californians under age 20 (465,000) than age 50 to 59 (71,000) were arrested for criminal offenses. In 2022, many fewer Californians under age 20 (48,000) than age 50 to 59 (84,000) were arrested for criminal offenses. While the figures presented here may seem unbelievable amid incessant media and institutional fear campaigns, they can be confirmed easily by perusing tables 16, 33, and 36 of *Crime in California 2021* (CDOJ, 2023).

Imagine a modern library system that receives 6 reports of disruptive behaviors by teenagers and 10 reports of disruptions by adults in their 50s (reflecting today's California crime patterns). Administrators typically *generalize* the teenaged disruptions to the entire young age group and consider restricting *all* teenagers' library privileges while *individualizing* more numerous disruptions by 50-agers as personal problems meriting personal, not collective, action. A crowd of middle-schoolers, particularly one containing darker-skinned youngsters, may be seen as a threat to order in and of itself. Many authorities seem to delight in mass bans and restrictions targeting youth and pick quarrels to justify them (e.g., "one butt to a chair" rules to police younger girls' tendency to sit close together) (Bernier & Males, 2014). Censorware unnecessarily restricts young people from communicating and obtaining information.

The oppressive, arbitrary treatment of teenagers by institutions, including libraries, results from the image of young people as a faceless mass defined by their worst-behaving fraction. A just model for young people is a system that addresses the guilty few without imposing collective guilt.

ARE TEENAGERS REALLY IN "CRISIS"?

Our thinking remains mired in a century-old past that regarded teens as reckless savages. Yet popular and official maladaptations should not prevent libraries from fully engaging new opportunities that challenge the destructive status quo. Libraries can play a key, if risky, role in reversing images that are constricting the opportunities of young people at a time they're showing dynamic, future-facing positives—including not just greatly improved behaviors but more tolerant and responsible political and social attitudes crucial to a multicultural world.

But why should simply acting on the stunningly hopeful truths about young people, which should delight a divided and troubled adult culture, be risky? Consider another misrepresented issue: the constantly proclaimed "teenage mental health crisis," into which libraries inevitably are drawn. The CDC's 2022 and 2023 surveillances find more 12- to 17-year-olds reporting depression and anxiety, captioned by the scary-sounding but meaningless refrain, "suicide is the second leading cause of death for adolescents."

As with most youth issues, perspective is cast to the winds (see Males, 2023b). First, authorities have declared a "mental health crisis" afflicting every younger generation, decade after decade, going back at least a century. Alarms were particularly loud over epidemics of "child suicide" in the 1910s, widespread youthful mental disorders revealed in 1930s surveys (what we now call "the greatest generation"), the 1970s and 1980s supposed "tripling in teen suicide" and widespread violence and drugs, the 1997 media-corrupted generation *Rolling Stone* branded America's "most damaged and disturbed" ever, the 2000s steady parade of "campus mental health crises" declared year after year . . . on and on.

Second, even if real, are more depression and anxiety among teenagers legitimate, healthy reactions to widespread depression, drug overdose, suicide, and abuses by adults around them? Compared to a high school–age youth, a 40-aged parent is 1.5 times more likely to be criminally arrested, twice as likely to commit suicide, and 10 times more likely to die from overdosing on alcohol or illicit drugs (including fentanyl) (CDC, n.d.). Adult depression tripled during the COVID pandemic, and the CDC's (2022) survey found 11 percent of youths reporting violent physical abuses and 55 percent reporting emotional abuses all at the hands of adults and caregivers—three to four times more than report bullying at school or online.

Yet leaders, professionals, and media evade the harsh realities many youths face and instead blame peers and social media. The most definitive study, by the Pew Research Center (2022), found very few teens find social media a negative experience. In addition, 80 percent said social media gives them some level of connection to what is going on in their friends' lives, 71 percent said it's a place where they can show their creativity, 67 percent said social media reassures them that they have people to support them during tough times, and 58 percent said it makes them feel more accepted (Pew Research Center, 2022).

LIBRARIES CAN CHALLENGE ANTI-YOUTH DISINFORMATION

As major institutions indulge widespread, irrational distortions, scapegoating, and restrictions threatening young people and America's social fabric, libraries can function as a powerful counterforce. By simply refusing to go along with the crusade against youths and young adults that panders to troubled older-generation prejudices, libraries can offer a dynamic new vision suited to the emerging multicultural society.

Libraries already have taken strong stances against censorship in defiance of popular and official crusades that can serve as a foundation for larger social campaigns. If just one major institution, forcefully committed to a fact-based campaign, tells the truth about American youth, pointedly fact-checking distortions and shaming institutions and media that indulge destructive falsehoods, its influence could be profound.

To what extent, then, do directors of library policies and media believe the statistics and trends shown in this chapter are factual, realistic representations? To what extent do they see basic library functions, such as free information provision, multimedia connections, and fact-based discourse, menaced by the larger, censorious anti-youth crusade founded in fear? The dramatic improvements in youth and young adult behaviors documented in this chapter affirm key progressive ideals, such as racial diversity, economic justice, and environmental health.

This is a new time. The fearsome "teenager" of legend has been replaced by the twenty-first-century teenager that little resembles outmoded stereotypes. While libraries don't command the power of political leaders or major media, they do have sufficient institutional standing to shake up the status quo with strongly documented, strongly worded dissents from today's factless narrative disparaging young people. When accompanied by policy stances upholding young people's rights to uncensored information and unhindered use of public spaces, libraries' fact-based advocacy can significantly challenge the stifling status quo. The best facts and realities support this challenge. The real question is whether libraries, particularly at contested local levels, have the will to speak truth to power.

DISCUSSION QUESTIONS

- In what ways might young adult library staff involve the "new" teenager in library services formation and evaluation?
- In what ways might young adult library staff share factual information about young adult behavioral issues for staff and the public?

- What information sources might library staff consult to remain current on youth adult behavioral trends?

REFERENCES

Bernier, A., & Males, M. (2014). *YA spaces and the end of postural tyranny.* Public Libraries. https://static1.squarespace.com/static/600e75a30eec4a7d0511f044/t/61aeb5ade602954e5da663ad/1638839726383/Bernierpercent2C+Males+percent28percent2714 percent29+Postural+Tyranny.pdf.

California Department of Justice (CDOJ). (2023). *Crime statistics.* https://openjustice.doj.ca.gov/exploration/crime-statistics.

Centers for Disease Control and Prevention (CDC). (n.d.). *CDC wonder.* https://wonder.cdc.gov/.

Centers for Disease Control and Prevention (CDC). (2022). *New CDC data illuminate youth mental health threats during the COVID-19 pandemic.* https://www.cdc.gov/media/releases/2022/p0331-youth-mental-health-covid-19.html.

Centers for Disease Control and Prevention (CDC). (2023). *Youth risk behavior survey.* https://www.cdc.gov/healthyyouth/data/yrbs/pdf/YRBS_Data-Summary-Trends_Report2023_508.pdf.

Males, M. (2023a, April 24). *Are U.S. schools dangerous places for gun violence?* Youth-Facts. https://www.youthfacts.org/?p=160964.

Males, M. (2023b, July 15). *We've gotten the "teenage mental health crisis" dangerously wrong.* Salon. https://www.salon.com/2023/07/15/weve-gotten-the-teenage-mental-health-crisis-dangerously/.

Nevin, R. (2021). *Plausibility: This is your brain on lead.* Ricknevin.com. https://ricknevin.com/plausibility-this-is-your-brain-on-lead/.

Pew Research Center. (2022). *Connection, creativity and drama: Teen life on social media in 2022.* https://www.pewresearch.org/internet/2022/11/16/connection-creativity-and-drama-teen-life-on-social-media-in-2022/.

Strang, N. M., Chein, J. M., & Steinberg L. (2013). The value of the dual systems model of adolescent risk-taking. *Frontiers.* https://www.frontiersin.org/articles/10.3389/fnhum.2013.00223/full#:~:text=This percent20perspective percent2C percent20referred percent20to percent20as percent20the percent20 percentE2 percent80 percent9Cdual percent20systems,age percent20period percent2C percent20but percent20that percent20develop percent20along percent20different percent20timetables.

Thomson, D., & Ryberg R. (2021). *Lessons from a historic decline in child poverty.* Child Trends. https://www.childtrends.org/publications/lessons-from-a-historic-decline-in-child-poverty.

US Census Bureau. (2023). *Tables.* https://data.census.gov/table?q=United+States&table=DP05&tid=ACSDP1Y2017.DP05&g=010XX00US&lastDisplayedRow=29&vintage=2017&layer=state&cid=DP05_0001E.

Part Three

Institutional Capacities and Models

16

Managing Up

CRITICAL LESSONS FOR INFLUENCE AND EFFECTIVENESS

Ken Haycock

Managing up is the art of taking control of the relationship between you and your boss. While it can be challenging, there are several strategies you can use to make it work.

But stop—really? How offensive is that proposition?

The language is a bit dated. "Managing up" suggests an element of manipulation and subterfuge. "Boss" or even "supervisor" suggests a hierarchical relationship based on power and close oversight.

This is not the reality of today's workplace (one hopes)—or we might reasonably label it unproductive at best and toxic at worst.

Managing up instead involves building a positive and productive relationship with your manager while meeting their expectations and needs. You want to work effectively with them and influence them in their decisions and in their support for you and young adult services.

Managing up is not about manipulating or controlling your boss. It's about a relationship that benefits both of you. It is aligning your goals and working with their expectations. It is about your agency, leadership, and ability to influence outcomes with authenticity and substance.

THE BASICS FROM MANAGEMENT

First, you need to understand your manager. Take the time to appreciate their preferences, communication style, and priorities. Learn about their expectations, strengths, and weaknesses. This knowledge will help you to tailor your approach and to collaborate better with them by fitting their needs.

Communicate to inform them of your progress, challenges, and successes. Be clear and concise in your communication. This can help build trust and prevent miscommunications or misunderstandings. Find the right balance between too much and too little. Seek their guidance and input when needed.

One suggestion, whether requested or not, is a one-page monthly report listing your accomplishments, meetings of note, professional development received or given, current issues or problems, and areas for discussion. And a few days later, ask to book an appointment to discuss your report. Be transparent in your interactions. This opens doors and establishes an ongoing basis for communication. No surprises.

You also need to understand what your manager cares about and their goals and priorities so you can align your work and communication. Anticipating their needs and preferences and taking the initiative to address them can help demonstrate your value and make their job easier.

Be a team player. Collaborate effectively. Building positive relationships with your manager and peers and fostering a cooperative work environment reflect well on your ability to manage and work with others. Recognize that compromise is often essential to long-term success.

Take on additional responsibilities, volunteer for challenging projects, and show initiative in driving positive change within your team or system. This demonstrates your commitment and dedication to overall success. Stepping up, stepping out, and assisting with issues beyond your area are critical to gaining support.

Only present an issue or challenge with a potential solution. This demonstrates your problem-solving abilities, positive attitude, and initiative. Feedback is essential to supervision and success, but there is a need for it to be better received. Ask for feedback on your work and how you can improve. Or better yet, ask for advice. "How could I have handled this situation differently?" "What would have been the effect of this approach?" "How can I make young adult services more central and visible in the system?" Be open to learning and growing, and identify areas for improvement; we all have them. Listen to their suggestions and incorporate them into your work.

ADDING LEADERSHIP AND INFLUENCE

There is often a dichotomy between management and leadership, but both are required to be effective—doing things right versus doing the right thing. Dealing with only one is limiting and less productive.

Leadership is about social influence, enlisting the engagement and support of others in achieving a common goal. This is the essence of a workplace relationship.

But how do you do it? To be influential, you must be self-aware, focused, and competent. This is also crucial to self-confidence, a key component to positive perceptions by others.

Influence can be defined as the ability to affect the behavior, thoughts, or actions of others.

Influence involves persuading someone to adopt a particular viewpoint or action. This can often be done through logical arguments and emotional appeals.

Influence is also associated with power. Those with more power can often exert more influence over others.

There are also lessons from research in advocacy—it is about respect (if for no other reason than that they hold the power); people do things for their reasons, not ours (so basic but so often forgotten). And advocacy is like banking; you can't make a withdrawal if you have never made a deposit (build the relationship and build understanding of your service over time).

SIX BASIC PRINCIPLES

The research from influence (see, for example, the work of Robert Cialdini, and as applied to politics and libraries, the work of Ken Haycock and Cheryl Stenstrom) demonstrates how six basic principles can advance your influence: liking, reciprocity, authority, social proof or consensus, commitment and consistency, and scarcity. Let's explore each of the six and the implications for your agency and influence.

To initiate, build, and repair relationships, consider liking and reciprocity:

1. *Liking*. Remember how to make friends and influence people? People tend to say yes when they like us and even more when they know we genuinely like them. You activate this by finding common ground for discussion (e.g., common personal characteristics and experiences or outlooks), offering praise when appropriate (be genuine) and amplifying it through cooperating. The euphemism "they are not a team player" tends to signify a lack of cooperation, a lack of "getting with the program." Find reasons to genuinely like your manager.

2. *Reciprocity*. People feel obligated when you give first. You, then me, then you, then me. To activate this principle, offer gifts. These are unexpected, custom, meaningful, and need not cost money. A simple yet powerful example would be to ask, "What are your major goals and priorities this year? How might I help to advance them?" Be sure to acknowledge your manager when appropriate and perhaps nominate them for awards. Invite them to special young adult events, recognize them. You also have a "moment of power" when you decide to back down or push harder (walk in or walk away), and each can work; walking away is not a sign of weakness.

And when receiving thanks, never say "no problem" but "I am happy to do it, and I know you would do the same for me."

In a period of uncertainty, appeal to authority and social proof (or consensus):

3. *Authority.* Your manager has authority and can support your initiatives. But you, too, have authority. You are a credible expert and can demonstrate your specialist knowledge as an unbiased source of information, so play the part. Dress professionally. Have an appropriate title and business card. Note your accomplishments in your monthly report. Establish your credibility through your expertise and trustworthiness, professionalism, industry knowledge, and credentials. And be secure enough to admit when you don't know. It pays off.

4. *Social proof or consensus.* Groups attract. Just as we have a cohort group of young adult specialists and attend conferences and workshops with them, your manager has a cohort of peers. They tend to do (as we do) what others like them are doing—and they contact their peers when uncertain. Provide examples and evidence of how others, in the same or other systems, feel, think, and act in similar settings and situations. Always focus on the behaviors that you want.

And finally, to move them to action, use commitment and consistency, and scarcity:

5. *Commitment and consistency.* This is critical to understanding your manager. What are their values and beliefs? The centrality of the public library in community building? Intellectual freedom? Social justice? Literacy for all? We are committed to our underlying principles. Our values guide us. We also want to be consistent with prior positions that we have taken. If you get a commitment, ask them to put it in writing ("Would you mind confirming that in an email so I have a record?"), or have them make a public statement (this engenders accountability). Don't corner or push anyone—if it is not voluntary, it won't last. Ask them to be consistent with prior decisions, actions, and statements.

6. *Scarcity.* The less there is, the more we want it. But would the loss of your young adult specialist position mean the service was not offered? Likely not, but not in the same way. What specifically would be lost? How would that have an impact on your community? It would help if you demonstrated unique or uncommon benefits not available elsewhere in your system or community.

A FEW BARRIERS

There are, of course, significant barriers to overcome to influence, but these are primarily attitudinal and preparatory.

The first barrier is the view that "it is not my job." This is a primary problem for those who do not believe that they should have to develop patterns of influence because they are a social and educational "good" and should be supported as such. Perhaps true, but the world does not work this way anymore (if indeed it ever did). Too often, these same professionals are the first to decry cuts in staffing and resources without having done anything to forestall them. They have neglected even simple advocacy—a planned, deliberate, and systematic approach to developing understanding and support incrementally over time—advocacy, not whining. One area of concern is the confusion of advocacy (e.g., showing respect and connecting agendas) with public relations or publicity (getting the message out). Talking is not influencing; talking is talking. Knowing your manager's "language" and their issues and concerns is essential. The second barrier to influence is the lack of a plan to enhance understanding and support. A valuable and important exercise is to assess the degree of leverage you already hold in your system and build a plan to increase understanding and support from your manager and colleagues. Do they have any background in young adult services and programs? Any positive experiences? Is their knowledge current? Based on evidence? How will you address any gaps over time?

There is no silver bullet or quick fix. Building influence means building relationships and building trust, and those take time. A realistic plan and a deep understanding of effective practices will enhance support over time.

We tend to rely too much on our experience and introspection (what would motivate me?) rather than developing a plan for others based on fact-finding.

KNOW YOURSELF

You need to know and understand your manager, of course. But what about you?

The first person you manage and lead is yourself. It is crucial to organize yourself to be efficient (this is necessary for survival and to allow you to give attention to what matters) and effective (to achieve your programmatic goals).

There are many tools available to help you develop a better understanding of yourself.

One common indicator used regularly for understanding type, temperament, and team development is the Myers-Briggs Type Indicator (MBTI). The MBTI reports some of your key preferences but certainly not all, and it does not look to stereotype or pigeonhole, only to develop understanding. And only you can decide how accurate any report is for you. Current objections to the MBTI tend to focus on its abuse rather than its effective use as a tool for self-knowledge.

Consider also, the Enneagram, another assessment tool. The MBTI tends to illustrate our preferred behaviors and approaches, while the Enneagram offers core motivations that shape those behaviors.

Another piece of this puzzle is identifying your specific organizational strengths. Few of us can articulate our strengths. We can outline our qualifications and our experiences, and we can even point to some significant accomplishments. But we need to be able to specify and articulate the underlying strengths that led to these actions.

Beginning with *Now, Discover Your Strengths*, several other approaches and contexts have been developed for "strengths-finding." Most provide a registration code in the book for an online assessment of your strengths. The *Buckingham and Clifton* assessment will provide you with your top 5 (of 34 possible) strengths and a description of each. The profile will also suggest ways the strength is typically used successfully in organizations and how each might be developed.

Identifying strengths helps you determine whether your current work environment and position help you work with your strengths (if not, you may find that this explains why you are unhappy in your position).

Knowing yourself allows you to challenge your excuses for not being successful. It enables you to analyze the situation more objectively to determine if there is a fit for you.

Only you can define your measures of personal success. Know yourself. Have a professional development plan. Continue to grow and develop.

SOME CONCLUSIONS

So, manage your boss?

Managing up involves building a positive and productive relationship with your manager while meeting their expectations and needs. You want to work effectively with them and influence them in their decisions and support.

So focus on the relationship, the approach you might use to understand them, communicate with them, and influence them.

What is their context? What are their issues? What are their primary goals this year where you might assist?

There is no one correct answer for every person and situation. But from our research, we conclude that "the relationship *is* the message." It is fundamental to your success.

So what? Now what? Only you can decide how deeply you believe in young people and their unique programs and services and the resulting need to develop a plan to exercise social influence.

Ken Haycock

Influence is a complex and multifaceted concept that involves a range of different characteristics. By understanding these key characteristics and deciding to apply them, developing more effective strategies for influencing others may be possible.

DISCUSSION QUESTIONS

- How does Haycock's definition of *advocacy* contrast with the notion of advocacy proposed by Sweeney (chapter 17)?
- How does Haycock's thesis comport with your own experiences with supervisors?

17

Understanding the Politics of Libraries in a Time of Book Banning

Patrick Sweeney

Collections and programming for youth in libraries are currently under attack. Over the past few years, we've seen a large-scale and coordinated movement to ban books from teen and children's collections and disrupt youth programming. We've watched as libraries are threatened with defunding due to the content of the books on the shelves of collections for youth. We have seen horrific legislative initiatives around books for youth, such as efforts to limit access to school library databases; proposals to establish book rating systems; mandating or prescribing materials challenge policies; efforts to regulate collection development policies; use of parental control policies to limit free speech; changes to obscenity and harmful to minors definitions that preempt First Amendment guarantees; bills that limit or outlaw the teaching of "divisive concepts"; and bills that would criminalize libraries, education, and museums by removing long-standing defense from prosecution exemptions under obscenity laws.

Many of these laws and local fights are being driven by organizations with extensive political power and influence. If youth librarians like you want to understand how to fight back, then you need to take the time to understand the political environment of libraries. You need to understand the basics of political power and influence. And you need to understand what it actually means to advocate for your collections and programs. If you're like me, none of this was taught to me in library school.

For example, did you know that 98 percent of library funding is political? If you look at the data from the Institute of Museum and Library Services (IMLS)

Public Library Survey you would see that over 90 percent of library funding comes from local voters and local legislators; 3 percent to 5 percent, from the state government; and 3 to 5 percent, from the federal government. That means that only 2 percent of library funding comes from philanthropic sources and from the fines and fees that libraries collect.

Yet when I graduated library school, I had no idea that library funding was so dependent on influencing politics. Not one course in library school taught me about the political nature of library funding. There were plenty of courses on grant writing, fundraising, and philanthropic funding for libraries. But again, that is only 2 percent of library funding. Nobody taught me how to address the other 98 percent of funding, and there were no courses available that focused on the political nature of library funding.

That's probably why, when I graduated, I took on a number of projects that I called "advocacy." For example, I sponsored the "Great Librarian Write-Out," where I encouraged librarians to write in nonlibrary publications about the role of libraries in American society. I also held a number of events, such as a freeze mob (remember those?), at a library conference in New Orleans. I even launched a project called the Story Sailboat, which brought books and reading programs, by boat, to communities around the San Francisco Bay and did "book seeding," where books were distributed that had nice things about libraries written on a book plate in the front jacket of the books. I even won a Movers & Shakers award from *Library Journal* for these "advocacy" projects. Yet not a single one of them was actually advocacy.

In fact, I'm exceptionally embarrassed by much of the "advocacy" work that I did once I graduated. I blame the industry that taught me that hanging "Libraries Transform" or "Geek the Library" posters above library drinking fountains was, in fact, advocacy. I was taught that if we just tell the public and our local, state, and federal legislators nice things about the library, then some magic will happen, and libraries will somehow gain the funding they need to survive. Unfortunately, that's just not how the world works.

Today, I work for an organization called EveryLibrary, which is a registered 501(c)(4) (nonprofit) that helps build voter support for libraries. In the last 10 years, we have provided pro bono support that has helped libraries win over 110 local ballot initiatives and brought in over 2.7 billion dollars in stable library funding. Our organization has also helped about as many school and public libraries keep their doors open when they were threatened with budget cuts from local and state legislators, and we are developing the tools, resources, and data that libraries need to be better advocates. Now, I have a much clearer understanding of what advocacy is and how it should be conducted to secure the resources that libraries need to continue to serve the public.

Nothing gets funded in the United States without political power and influence. If causes received funding or government support strictly because they were good for society, we would live in a much different world than we do now.

We would probably have cures for more diseases, less homeless and hungry individuals, and less unsupported individuals who are impacted by mental health issues, and our students would be far more educated and competitive in the global job market. But that's simply not the case, and it's not the case simply because those causes and issues don't have the political power and influence they need to be resolved.

Political power and influence comes from only two sources in the library industry: our associations, advocacy organizations, and other affiliated organizations have never done any work to cultivate those two sources. This power and influence comes from people and money. Whichever cause has the most people or the most money is the one that wins regardless of that cause's impact on our society. For good or bad, they will win.

With enough people, a cause can launch a "people-powered" movement. One of the organizations that we are probably most familiar with is the National Rifle Association (NRA). The reason that we can't move conversations forward around the Second Amendment is because the NRA has a contactable database of millions of voters across the country. That database (or voter file) contains dozens, if not hundreds, of data points on each of these voters. They know which ones believe in the Second Amendment, and which ones don't. This is how they know who to contact and who to avoid, which helps them to conserve resources by only contacting the people that are on their side. They also know the messages to which each of those voters will respond. For example, they know if the voter responds to messages around getting guns taken away, or messages around freedom and liberty, or messages around public safety or "stand-your-ground" laws. They also know if that voter responds to direct mail, phone calls, canvassing, social media ads, or other paid or earned media. That means that if a legislator comments on gun rights, the NRA can immediately reach out to hundreds of thousands of voters in that legislator's district to tell them whether that legislator supports or opposes the Second Amendment, and they can do so using a medium with which the voter engages. That's political power and influence using people.

To be fair, hundreds of organizations function like the NRA. The NRA is simply the easiest to highlight. Those people-powered organizations include the Sierra Club, Human Rights Campaign, Planned Parenthood, the Republican National Committee and the Democratic National Committee, Extinction Rebellion, Indivisible, Moms for Liberty, Black Lives Matter, Standing Rock, and many more. This is simply how sophisticated causes that understand political power and influence utilize people to push an agenda forward.

On the other hand, organizations such as the American Legislative Exchange Council (ALEC), which lobbies for corporate rights, are extremely well funded by those same corporations. ALEC uses this money to make campaign contributions; contributions to causes that support various candidates; and as we've seen with the individuals on the Supreme Court, it has the ability to pay off debts, purchase houses, and pay the "consulting fees" to legislators, members of the judiciary, and their spouses. This allows ALEC to gain direct access to individuals in positions of power and to propose model legislation or sway judiciary outcomes. This is political power through money.

We are currently seeing the same kinds of fights for political power play out at the local level. Organizations such as Patriot Mobile (money) and Moms for Liberty (people) are turning their resources out to influence local legislators or to get their own preferred candidates elected to office, who will then be beholden to the whims of these organizations due to their dependence on those organizations for the resources the legislators need to stay in office. And not only are they winning, but they are coming after libraries and attacking them through proposed pieces of legislation that would allow for the incarceration of librarians, the banning of books, and the defunding of thousands of libraries across the country.

They can do this because libraries have zero political power and influence. Librarians and libraries have neither money nor a national voter file because those in leadership positions have never done any of the work necessary to build the resources that our side needs to win. This is why I now say that an activity is not advocacy unless it identifies supporters or raises money. And none of the activities that I was rewarded for in the beginning of my career should have been counted as advocacy.

While raising the funding that libraries need to have political power and influence is probably a long shot, libraries, associations, and our advocacy organizations can most likely build a people-powered movement to help move a pro-library agenda forward. This kind of campaign can help support pro-library legislation or be used to fight against anti-library legislation. But to do so, we need a national voter file of millions of Americans who support libraries, and the only organization currently building such a voter file is EveryLibrary. And to build a national voter file, we need the data to make it less costly to identify our supporters.

OCLC conducted the first comprehensive study of the views of voters and legislators in their "Awareness to Funding" reports, the first of which was conducted in 2008 and the second, in 2018. This means that these were also the first longitudinal studies of political sentiments of voters and legislators. I want to make clear how preposterous it is, even though 98 percent of library funding is political in nature, that we, as an industry, have only comprehensively and longitudinally looked at the political sentiments that directly affect our funding twice in over a hundred years of existence. Twice. These reports were critical because they highlighted some keen insights such as the following:

- Voters on the both ends of political spectrum are just as likely to vote for or against library funding.

- There is zero correlation between a library user and a library supporter, which means that library users are just as likely to vote for or against funding for the library as nonusers.
- There is no correlation between library card-holders rates and the likelihood that a library will win or lose a local election.
- Super supporters, which made up 6.5 percent of the population in 2018, rate libraries 9 percent better than they did in 2008 but are 16 percent less likely to vote for them.
- Libraries lost between 14 and 20 percent of voter support between 2008 and 2018, which should be a wake-up call to librarians across the country.

However, as critical as this study was, it also missed a number of incredibly important points. This report doesn't tell us who votes for libraries or why. It doesn't tell us the demographic nature of library voters, so we can't use this data to target voters who are on our side. It also doesn't tell us which demographic of voters are more or less likely to respond to various messages or through various media. This means that although we had some keen insights, we are lacking the kinds of data that we need to launch a people-powered movement in the same way that organizations like the NRA are able to.

One point that the report got very close to correct was the following callout:

Cultivate and Empower Super Supporters

A significant bright spot in the research is that support among library Super Supporters—a small but mighty group—is largely unchanged. This segment's loyalty should not be taken for granted, but rather nurtured and protected. In addition, library leaders can consider how to engage and leverage this group as library ambassadors to advocate with decision makers and influence other segments of the population that might be more disconnected or skeptical.

What this callout failed to highlight is that we need to "identify" who our super supporters are if we want to be able to cultivate and empower them. It should read, "*Identify*, Cultivate, and Empower Super Supporters," because obviously, how can we cultivate someone if we don't know who they are in our communities?

You're probably thinking that it seems like a daunting task to cultivate and empower the majority of the public into supporting libraries. However, we don't need to do that. A study by Harvard sociologist Erica Chenoweth and M. J. Stephan (2008) found that it takes only around 3.5 percent of the population actively participating in actions to ensure serious political change. In fact, they found that any movement that actively engaged just 3.5 percent of the public has never failed. And luckily, as we saw in the Awareness to Funding study, libraries have at least 6.5 percent of the public as super supporters, or those who will be most likely to actively engage.

What this means is that we have a clear path to winning if only we take the time to rethink our current definition of advocacy. We can't reward activities that do not identify supporters or raise money with awards and call that advocacy. True advocacy happens only when we are building the resources that we need to influence politics and the very foundation of our sources of funding. We need to take the time to identify our supporters and cultivate them into action through concrete actions using more sophisticated political tools and resources. We need to create a people-powered movement for libraries and to be comfortable recognizing that anything that doesn't lead to that goal is not advocacy.

DISCUSSION QUESTIONS

- In what ways might young adults be mobilized to identify super supporters for library advocacy?
- If 16- and 17-year-olds were allowed to vote in local elections, and based on current conventional levels of young adult services, to what degree would they/should they support library funding?
- What sources of factual information might libraries consult in assembling effective advocacy and support?

REFERENCE

Chenoweth, E., & Stephan, M. J. (2008). Why civil resistance works: The strategic logic of nonviolent conflict. *International Security*, *33*(1), 7–44. https://doi.org/10.1162/isec.2008.33.1.7.

18

Youth Services in Public and School Libraries

HISTORICAL CONSTRAINTS = CONTEMPORARY CHALLENGES

Wayne A. Wiegand

In late 1957 in rural Arkansas, 16-year-old Olly Neal—"a poor black kid with an attitude"—cut a class at his racially segregated school during his senior year and wandered into the library managed by Mildred Grady, a Black English teacher he had previously brought to tears with his disrespectful behavior. There his eye caught a book with a sexy woman on the cover, a practice pulp paperback publishers used commonly in the 1950s to sell series fiction. The book was titled *The Treasure of Pleasant Valley* by Black author Frank Yerby. Because he didn't want his classmates to know he was reading a novel, Neal chose to steal the book, rather than check it out, and took it home. There he had a transformative reading experience and found himself loving the book. He sneaked it back into its rightful place in the fiction section of the library, where he found yet another Yerby, which he also stole. Twice more this happened, and gradually, Neal began picking up other books. "Reading got to be a thing I liked."

After graduation, Neal went on to college; then law school; and in 1991, became Arkansas's first Black district attorney; then a judge; and later, an appellate court judge. At his 1970 high school reunion, however, Mildred Grady approached Neal and told him she had seen him steal the book back in 1957 but thought better of confronting him. Instead, she drove 70 miles to Memphis to find another Yerby and twice more made the trip as Neal repeated his thefts, each time purchasing the books with her own money and "all in hopes of turning around a rude adolescent who had made her cry," wrote Nicholas Kristof (2012) in a *New York Times* op-ed piece. "I credit Mrs. Grady for getting me in the habit of reading so that I was able to go to law school and survive," Neal told National Public Radio (StoryCorps, 2009).

I discovered this anecdote in research for my latest book, *American Public School Librarianship: A History* (Wiegand, 2021), and repeat it here for a reason. Youth services in public and school libraries has a history of about 125 years, so the anecdote about Mildred Grady and Olly Neal is chronologically about halfway between. And although it appears to be a happy story, it masks many obstacles and biases Grady had to overcome just to get *The Treasure of Pleasant Valley* on her library shelves. These obstacles and biases still dog youth services librarians in public and school libraries today. Let me detail several.

More than 90 percent of American public and school library collections are still governed by the Dewey Decimal Classification (DDC) system, a form of organization crafted on the Amherst College campus between 1874 and 1876. From its beginnings DDC manifested the White Anglo-Saxon Protestant heterosexual male biases of that campus and the person who put it together. It also focused only on what, at the time, was called "useful knowledge." In Melvil Dewey's mind, fiction was simply not important enough to occupy a cataloger's attention.

That attitude toward fiction manifested itself in other ways. Literary establishment leaders, who were Dewey's contemporaries (the vast majority of whom were WASP [white, Anglo-Saxon Protestant] male heterosexuals) divided fiction into two categories—"serious" and "leisure" (later "recreational")—and claimed authority to know the difference between the two. In their major media reviews, they ardently advocated for the former and generally disparaged the latter. A case in point is what Nathaniel Hawthorne called that "d----d mob of scribbling women" who were outselling him in 1855. Pushed by these literary authorities, serious fiction found its way into public school curricula. Categories of the much more popular "genrefiction" (note the judgmental prefix literary authorities had crafted), such as "mystery," "western," "science fiction," "fantasy," and "romance," did not.

By 1957, librarianship had also come to rely on a number of acquisition guides such as *Children's Catalog* and *Public Library Catalog*, and periodicals such as *Booklist* and *Horn Book*. Like the DDC, all manifested a white world bias and privileged titles issued by the largely white publishing world that early on recognized ways to get their books listed in these guides. "Advising" Mildred Grady's collection was the *Senior High School Library Catalog* (*SHSLC*), a quinquennial guide of 5,000 titles published by the H. W. Wilson Company. A group of about 25 mostly female white volunteer high school librarians advised Wilson about which titles to include. Many state departments of education, Arkansas included, also crafted lists of titles for state school libraries and often provided matching funds for schools that made their selections based on these guides. For a variety of reasons made obvious in the paragraphs above, Black author Frank Yerby was not in *SHSLC* nor on the Arkansas list, so to acquire his books, Mildred Grady not only had to buck conventional library practice and the authorities it followed; she also had to make an extraordinary effort to acquire Yerby titles.

And then there was the Jim Crow environment in which Grady had to work. At the time, the Supreme Court's 1954 *Brown v. Board of Education* decision declaring that racially segregated schools were separate but not equal and therefore illegal, was being periodically tested across the South. Nowhere was this more intense than the integration efforts in the fall of 1957 by nine Black students at the white Central High School of Little Rock, 100 miles to her west. Grady must have known of the violence caused by white reaction that for several months saturated national news; she probably did not want that violence visited on her town.

Another element that shaped her professional environment was funding. At the time, the white-run state departments of education in the Jim Crow South were routinely underfunding Black schools, and that situation was also evident in the high school library, for which Grady was responsible. Like most other states, Arkansas had minimum standards for high schools to meet in order to qualify for accreditation, and supporting some kind of a library was among them. Stretching budgets by routinely buying recommended books that qualified for matching state funds was one way to meet standards. Another was staffing, but because Jim Crow states routinely underfunded education, accrediting agencies across the South often allowed underfunded high schools to assign someone from the regular faculty—usually an English teacher—to manage the school library part-time. Because of funding inequities, this happened more often in Black than white high schools. Such was Mildred Grady's case, and she gave as much time to the library and did the best she could, given the Jim Crow circumstances in which she found herself. This included acquiring Black authors overlooked in standard acquisitions guides for the Black students she served. When Olly Neal "stole" her only Yerby, she felt compelled to drive to Memphis several times and use her own money to obtain other books by this Black author.

Other obstacles and racial biases, over which she had no control, also existed in Mildred Grady's library. In 1901, the H. W. Wilson Company began issuing the *Readers' Guide to Periodical Literature (RGPL)* to make the contents of magazines, subscribed to in the growing number of public libraries across the country, easier to retrieve. Initially, it indexed 20 popular periodicals, almost all edited by cultural authorities north of the Mason-Dixon Line, who were dedicated to publishing material fitting the canons of the WASP upper- and middle-class male culture, in which most of them lived. To counter these kinds of racial biases, literary historian Elizabeth McHenry notes, reasonably popular Black authors such as Charles Chesnutt and Paul Lawrence Dunbar routinely altered their literary creations to meet the expectations of their white editors (McHenry, 2021).

Mary Church Terrell, herself a prolific early twentieth-century Black author of short stories that white editors mostly refused to print, called this situation a "conspiracy of silence." "No one wants a story about a Negro," she complained in her journal in 1906. When she asked the editor of *American Magazine* "if he thought his or any other publication would accept a modern version of *Uncle Tom's Cabin*" that "depicted the injustice commonly perpetrated upon colored people all over the United States," he responded that "no periodical in the country would publish any such story at that time." From these kinds of responses, Terrell concluded that only authors who made Black Americans look "ridiculous or criminal can get a hearing in the press," but Black Americans' "trials and struggles and heart aches are tabooed. . . . Be sure to let your brothers and sisters of a darker hue alone, unless you make them monkeys or criminals" (McHenry, 2021, pp. 8–9).

And like the white periodicals it indexed (*American Magazine* included), *RGPL* automatically reinforced racial biases. In his study of the portrayal of Black Americans in these turn-of-the-century leading periodicals, historian Rayford Logan notes how these "devotees to the Genteel Tradition found such evident delight in the lampooning of Negroes" (Logan, 1954, p. 240). The "new media were spreading racial stereotypes nationally," as popular magazines such as *Harper's Weekly*, *Atlantic Monthly*, and *Century Magazine* "published short fiction, poetry, travel accounts, and cartoons that showed Black people as crude and grotesque," writes Charles Reagan Wilson (2022, p. 142). "Gross humor made laughing at Black people a norm. Popular culture depicted Black people as savage, bestial looking, dishonest, idle, and criminal" (Wilson, 2022, p. 142).

In 1937, the Wilson Company began issuing the *Abridged Readers' Guide to Periodical Literature* (*ARGPL*), which covered 20 periodicals available in most school libraries. To speed student access to the information these periodicals contained, school librarians generally subscribed to as many *ARGPL* indexed periodicals as their budgets permitted. Although millions of Black students attended thousands of Black high schools across the country, in 1957 *ARGPL* indexed no Black periodical—not *Negro History Bulletin*, a monthly newsletter published since 1937 by Carter Woodson's Association for the Study of Negro Life and History nor *Negro Digest* (established in 1942), *Ebony* (1945), or *Jet: The Weekly Negro News Magazine* (1951), all of which graced the coffee tables of many middle-class Black homes and boasted circulation rates higher than several of the white periodicals Wilson did index.

Had senior high school student Olly Neal undertaken a writing assignment on mid-century Black authors, he would have found little information using *ARGPL*. On the other hand, *ARGPL* did index *National Geographic*, which until the 1960s, its editor readily admitted in 2018, not only "all but ignored people of color who lived in the United States, rarely acknowledging them beyond laborers and domestic workers" (Hawkins, 2018, para. 4); it also depicted Black people elsewhere in the world "as exotics, famously and frequently unclothed, happy hunters, noble savages—every type of cliché" (Hawkins, 2018, para. 4). In 1962, Black seventh-grader Karen Holloway noticed "the magazine dared to photograph people as objects, and the people looked like me without my clothes on" (Holloway, 2006, p. 3).

The obstacles Mildred Grady had to overcome and the biases she had to quietly contest in 1957 to put Frank Yerby titles on her school library shelves may have shifted in the last 60 years, but they have hardly disappeared. Race, class, gender, ageist, and heterosexual biases (among others) still exist among authorities who control the funding of public and school libraries and influence the local political and educational environments in which youth services librarians have to practice their professional responsibilities. And unfortunately, some of these obstacles and biases are still systemic in the traditional acquisition routines youth services librarians follow and the information services they provide.

All of this creates constraints for contemporary youth services librarians not unlike those Mildred Grady confronted in 1957. Given the circumstances in which she found herself, she confronted these constraints as best she could, and for Olly Neal, her efforts paid large dividends. Hopefully, the record of her experiences I detail here can provide a model for contemporary youth services librarians called upon to meet the challenges of the present. The challenge for contemporary youth services librarians is to identify the obstacles and biases affecting their professional practice and—like Mildred Grady—address them as best they can given the environments and circumstances in which they work. The Olly Neals of the future will thank them.

DISCUSSION QUESTIONS

- How does learning about this history of library services affect your view of the profession?
- What other historical questions deserve to be asked about young adult services?
- What sources of primary records would be useful in furthering the study of young adult library services history?

REFERENCES

Hawkins, D. (2018, March 13). National Geographic confronts its past: "For decades, our coverage was racist." *Washington Post*. https://www.washingtonpost.com/news/morning-mix/wp/2018/03/13/national-geographic-confronts-its-past-for-decades-our-coverage-was-racist/.

Holloway, K. (2006). *BookMarks: Reading in black and white*. Rutgers University Press.

Kristof, N. D. (2012, January 22). How Mrs. Grady transformed Olly Neal. *New York Times*, Section SR, 13.

Logan, R. W. (1954). *The Negro in American life and thought: The nadir, 1877-1901*. Dial.

McHenry, E. (2021). *To make Negro literature: Writing, literary practice, and African American authorship*. Duke University Press.

StoryCorps. (2009, October 2). *Boy lifts book; librarian changes boy's life*. NPR. https://www.npr.org/templates/story/story.php?storyId=113357239.

Wiegand, W. A. (2021). *American public school librarianship: A history*. Johns Hopkins University Press.

Wilson, C. R. (2022). *The Southern way of life: Meanings of culture and civilization in the American South*. University of North Carolina Press.

19

Overcoming Erasure

THE FIRST YOUNG ADULT LIBRARY SPACE

Anthony Bernier

The City of Los Angeles erupted in violence in 1992. One year after police had mercilessly beaten unarmed Black motorist Rodney King, as acquittals of the four involved Los Angeles Police Department (LAPD) officers rang out, rioting spread across the city. The subsequent week of insurrection and the media's fallacious depiction of young peoples' responsibility for it awakened in this librarian a critical awareness about how libraries were inadequately serving young adults. Wasn't the library supposed to be about *supporting* young people?

This chapter encapsulates the challenge I faced in implementing a new and more responsive library role for young adult services at the Los Angeles Public Library (LAPL) as well as the opportunities I pursued in addressing it. What resulted was the nation's first purpose-built young adult library space: Teen'Scape.

Six years before the Los Angeles riots, in the spring of 1986, LAPL's Central Library suffered the largest fire in US library history. Seven years and 150 million dollars later, the renovation included a 330,000-square-foot expansion featuring custom furniture, custom carpeting, and world-class public art when it reopened to nationwide acclaim.

When it did reopen in the fall of 1993, however, not an inch of those additional 330,000 square feet directly served the city's young adults. Indeed, senior management reputedly *erased* even the shelving of young adult materials from the architectural blueprints.

Of course, "erasing" young adults from library space, I later learned, was nothing new. Without traditional advocates enjoyed by children and adult services, libraries seldom account for young adult services and have devoted more space and design consideration to restrooms than to teenage users. The practice continues to the present day. As historian Abigail Van Slyke has written, space and young people have been a problem in libraries since the nineteenth century.

Librarians may complain about too many (or too few) teenagers but never about the floor plans erasing them. Among many other culture-wide prohibitions against young people, I long ago coined the term "Geography of No" to reflect library complicity in erasing young people from its public space and civic infrastructure.

In the wake of both the 1992 riots and the extravagant Central Library renovation unveiled in 1993, I developed a critique of young adult library services and began presenting administration a philosophical argument highlighting the absence of any space in the entire Central Library where young adults could feel welcome.

Fortunately, LAPL was at that time headed by progressive firebrand City Librarian Elizabeth Martinez. Persuaded by my analysis, Martinez (prior to being named executive director of the American Library Association) appointed me project manager; reassigned me from branches to Central Library; and allowed me to recruit Ann Hoffman, another experienced young adult librarian, to collaborate with me in pursuing a broader young adult vision.

Oddly, and despite seven years of planning, the costly Central Library renovation failed to find a purpose for a space adjacent to the building's historic rotunda. That was where we set up shop and began addressing the spatial inequity the library inflicted on the city's young adults.

The plan's modest goal to implement some spatial equity for young adults, however, became a bigger challenge than anticipated. We dutifully conducted literature searches and examined LAPL's archives. We inquired with colleagues in other large city libraries. We questioned library architects. We quickly discovered that libraries had been ignoring young adult spatial needs systemically and historically.

There were no models. There was no "best practices" literature. Library and information science (LIS) textbooks did not, and *still* do not, mention young adult spaces. We found no library expertise to draw upon.[1] Our research did, of course, identify books about library spaces (written by architects and designers relying on experience but not research). None took young adult space seriously. None involved young adult participation in the design process. While we did find rare evidence of libraries setting aside ad hoc collections and bargain basement shelving units for young adult materials, there was no record of a *purposefully designed* library space for young adults and not one example of young adult participation in any design process.

Our vision endeavored to correct how the library erased them from library space and reimagine a new and active role for their participation in the design process. Further, we assumed the library would value this vision—as a progressive innovation and contribution to the field.

Anthony Bernier

We next conducted research on methods for designing a process capable of incorporating youth participation. Here, we found models in the disciplines of anthropology and critical youth studies—both advocated systematic youth participation in research and civic engagement.

We then prospected high schools throughout the city, as well as youth organizations, alternative schools, and youth services, such as maternity homes and homeless youth shelters, to recruit "delegates" for a "Teen Town Hall." Fifty teen representatives from all over the city came together on May 14, 1994: the largest young adult event ever held in the Central's formal auditorium. The agenda included a critique of how young people had been erased from the renovation, solicited ideas for a new vision and space, and helped delegates discuss and prioritize plausible options for the *first purpose-built* library space for young adults.

In preparation for the Teen Town Hall, we rehearsed a nonprofit youth leadership organization to run registration and facilitate small design focus groups called *charettes*. We outfitted them with large pads and easels. Chicano civil rights hero and teacher Sal Castro inspired the delegates with his keynote address, acknowledging the event as "The First Teen Continental Congress." For entertainment, youth delegates played two rounds of *The Dating Game*, hosted by a local radio personality. Delegates also voted for the space's unusual name—"Teen'Scape"—to unequivocally denote age specificity (reinforced by a possessive apostrophe) and emphasize its physical square footage: "land*scape*."

Introducing the new space at Central Library naturally required constant communication with other departments and personnel. Archival records contain detailed memos, drafts, and revisions of planning documents, resource lists, and communications to and from managers, administrators, and staff.

Despite our efforts to involve and inform library staff, however, the initiative faced significant and lingering resistance. We might have anticipated that a modicum of reluctance would be interpreted as criticism of the costly renovation. And to some extent it was.

But resistance came in many forms, especially as new executive library leadership assumed office. A new space design plan was forbidden to be circulated. New furniture was forbidden (only leftover pieces, such as a single 1926 antique display unit). No marketing or announcement was allowed. No reports to the Library Commission or Library Friends. Administration summarily canceled meetings. The wealthy LAPL Foundation denied a 250 dollar request for pizza and soda for the Town Hall delegates. The library's volunteer office, likewise, denied a request for keepsake bookmarks (gifted to other volunteers). Other staff resistance and resentment manifested socially in "cold shoulders" and delays in following through with promised tasks.

Indeed, five years passed before Teen'Scape even appeared on the building directory.

Despite these institutional obstructions, however, success mounted quickly in this "biblio-beachhead." In particular, the innovation achieved progress with collections. In addition to high-interest, curricular support and reference materials brought together from various library departments, we purchased hundreds of new music CDs and multiple copies of the latest fiction and nonfiction as well as amassed the broadest collection of young adult–interest magazines available anywhere. The new space offered four computers, where young adults had access to none before. And we loaded them with the latest high-interest programs.

Stakeholders and library staff eventually warmed to the Teen'Scape vision through the ways in which young people responded as a legitimate service population. Contemporary records document a 26 percent jump in computer usage between 1997 and 1998 alone, along with unheard-of spikes in young adult fiction and nonfiction circulation. These metrics, along with growing internal acceptance and most importantly, external support from youth organizations, schools, parents, and local media, eventually drew the attention of the LAPL Foundation's Board of Directors, who began to see the project's public service value.

Based on this success, my associate Ann and I began transposing an expanded plan for a better-supported and permanent institutional commitment to young adult services. Together in consultation with young people, youth service providers, teachers, library staff, and administration, that plan eventually guided a professional architect through enacting what became the first permanent and *purpose-built* young adult library space called Teen'Scape.

When the fully appointed Teen'Scape Department opened on March 14, 2000, it spread across 3,780 square feet and unquestionably boasted the largest, most technically sophisticated, best selected young adult collection of any library in the nation.

Teen'Scape now occupied six separate "zones," including playful and techno-savvy collaborative workspaces, café tables with 19 flat-screen terminals connected to the internet, over 500 databases, and wall alcoves for private music enjoyment. Three canvas-roofed small group spaces opened to a state-of-the-art "Living Room" featuring a huge TV screen and plush sofas and movable lounge furniture, and life-size blowups of Spiderman, Buffy the Vampire Slayer, and Yoda appeared throughout.

In addition to all the fun, Teen'Scape also offered a well-equipped reference station and eight dedicated word-processing computers, open shelving access to 30,000 volumes, over 150 magazines (many international titles), graphic novels, videos, and CDs, not to mention serving as a launchpad to the rest of Central Library's world-class holdings and the almost 6 million items housed throughout LAPL's expansive 67 branch system.

The *Los Angeles Times* article celebrated Teen'Scape's opening, quoting one youth's response, "This is *way* off the scale. It's like landing on Mars!"

While today's Teen'Scape now serves as a powerful rejoinder to the resistance and cynicism we experienced during the project's development, I wish this story ended on a happier note. I wish, for example, the LAPL had taken pride in developing the first purpose-built young adult library space the way the *Los Angeles Times* or the *Downtown News* heralded it, or as it was featured in such popular media as *Archie Comics* and *Street Beat* magazine. I wish the LAPL had envisioned Teen'Scape as a much-needed training ground for new young adult professionals. And I wish the rest of the field could have looked to Teen'Scape as a model for working deeply and thoroughly with young people in space design processes.

Instead, as research I have published elsewhere documents, when libraries consider young adults at all, even under the best circumstance, they may bring staff together with architects and perhaps young adults as afterthoughts. What ensues, however, is what I have termed "The Naïve Triangle": architects, who frequently know little about the functioning of libraries or how young people enact public space; librarians, who generally do not possess architectural backgrounds and do not know a great deal about young people and spatiality; and young people (if they are involved at all), who participate with little preparation about library functioning or architectural requirements.

In contrast, the Teen'Scape project enacted a transparent process thoroughly involving stakeholders *informed by choices possible under given circumstances* to benefit from everyone's meaningful input.

Yet The Naïve Triangle persists. Aside from bright wall colors, a big "Teens" sign, and perhaps a few READ posters, libraries continue to enact mediocre young adult spaces conventionally indistinguishable from other spaces.

Despite these continuing challenges, however, and in contrast to traditional erasure, anecdotal evidence today suggests that libraries are finally accommodating some notion of young adult space. Since Teen'Scape, all new and renovated LAPL branches include at least a gesture toward young adult space equity. And while LAPL did not initially take pride in this advance in library services, two large public libraries (Phoenix Public Library and Chicago Public Library's YouMedia Center) more quickly adopted and called attention to their own subsequent versions. A few other libraries have followed. My own work as a scholar, too, continues to advocate for young adult space equity through teaching, research, and consulting. Collectively, these are no small accomplishments.

Taken together, the history of Teen'Scape's origins reflect the challenges presented by traditional anti-youth culture and institutional practice resulting in the erased needs of young adult library users. But it also stands as an object lesson in persistence and innovation in advancing service equity through the incorporation of young people as legitimate community members and contributors, not simply passive or invisible library service consumers.

DISCUSSION QUESTIONS

- What steps or resources would you consider if tasked with bringing about institutional change in young adult services?
- What factors contributed to the changes in staff perception about this new feature of young adult services?
- To what degree do young adults really need separate young adult spaces in libraries?

NOTE

1. Indeed, the first and only doctoral research was not produced until 2009: Shari A. Lee, "Teen Space: Designed for Whom?," unpublished doctoral dissertation, 2009, University of California, Los Angeles. The Young Adult Library Services Association (Young Adult LSA) did not produce its National Teen Space Guidelines until 2012, though little of what appears in them is supported with evidence.

REFERENCES

Agosto, D., Kuhlmann, M. L., Pacheco Bell, J., & Bernier, A. (2014, May/June). Learning from libraries and teens about young adult library spaces. *Public Libraries, 53*(3), 24-28.

Bernier, A. (1998, October). Bathrooms, bedrooms, and young adult spaces. *American Libraries, 29*(9), 52.

Bernier, A. (2000, February). Young adults, rituals, and library space. *Voice of Youth Advocates, 26*(3).

Bernier, A. (2003). Young adult space: The final frontier. In K. Worman (Ed.), *Young adult services institute: Serving San Joaquin Valley teens in the 21st century.* San Joaquin Valley Library System.

Bernier, A. (2009, September/October). "A space for myself to go": Early patterns in small young adult spaces. *Public Libraries, 48*(5), 33-47.

Bernier, A. (2010). Spacing out with young adults: Translating young adult space concepts back into practice. In D. E. Agosto & S. Hughes-Hassell (Eds.), *The information needs and behaviors of urban teens: Research and practice* (pp. 113-26). ALA Editions.

Bernier, A. (2010, May). Ten years of YA Spaces of Your Dreams: What have we learned? *Voice of Youth Advocates.* https://web.archive.org/web/20210717231711/http://voyamagazine.com/2010/05/13/ten-years-of-ya-spaces-of-your-dreams-what-have-we-learned/.

Bernier, A. (2012). *VOYA's YA Spaces of Your Dreams collection.* VOYA Press.

Bernier, A., Males, M., & Rickman, C. (2014, April). "It is silly to hide your most active patrons": Exploring user participation of library space designs for young adults in the United States. *Library Quarterly: Information, Community, Policy, 84,* 1-18.

Bernier, A., & Males, M. (2014, July/August). Young adult spaces and the end of postural tyranny. *Public Libraries, 53*(4), 30-40.

20

VOYA

THE MOTIVATIONAL MAGAZINE

Dina Schuldner

As you work toward becoming a young adult librarian or developing yourself as a practitioner, consider the impact that your work can have not only on your career or your ability to put food on the table but also on the lives of young adults. Your work can give young adults the ability to shape their own futures outside of gangs, crushing college debt, becoming parents before they are grown themselves, drug abuse, or allowing social media to limit their personal growth. The power of connection keeps young adults engaged. Similarly, young adult librarians need to be connected as they grow with and serve their communities. When I was in library school, there existed a forum for young adult librarians to share their research and successes in programming. It was independent of the American Library Association (ALA). Striving for inclusion as a student and eventually, practitioner catapulted me to becoming a highly impactful young adult librarian. This forum was the *Voice of Youth Advocates* (*VOYA*), which unfortunately, is now defunct. Resurrecting it, or creating a similar iteration of it, would inspire highly motivated students to become impactful in service to young adults in the public library.

In 2011, during my fourth semester of the graduate library science program at Queens College in New York City, I was approached by my professor of Young Adult Services to submit my paper for publication in *VOYA*, the trade magazine she had founded along with Dorothy Broderick in the 1970s. As an aspiring young adult librarian, I couldn't have been asked a more important question. To me, hearing that Mary K. Chelton thought my work was important enough to be shared with practicing, accomplished, successful young adult librarians was such an honor, a privilege, and a compliment that it gave me the belief that I could be like her—a young adult librarian who could make a significant contribution to the profession.

The previous year, Dr. Chelton had invited me to a luncheon in her honor, hosted by *VOYA*, at the ALA Annual Conference in Washington, DC (my first and only ALA Annual Conference in my, so far, 13 years in the profession). There, I met Dr. David Loertscher; Dr. Anthony Bernier; and RoseMary Honnold (now Ludt), the former editor of *VOYA*. We all had a friendly chat, and I couldn't believe that I was in the company of such intellectual powerhouses—just chatting about things we found interesting and important.

For me, *VOYA* simultaneously represented the gateway and the destination to a profession that would become my life's passion as I forged my path to becoming a young adult librarian at the Gold Coast Public Library in Glen Head, New York.

My first article in the magazine was published in August 2011; it was titled *Afraid to Be Fat: Eating Disorders and Young Adults*. In my Young Adult Services class, Dr. Chelton had charged us with compiling an annotated bibliography that addressed an information need of young adults. Having no idea what young adults were interested in at the time, I visited a public library close to me, the Shelter Rock Public Library in Searingtown, New York. I toured the library's young adult section and took a moment to ask the librarian if she would share some of the questions young adults have asked her as well as some of the topics they were interested in researching. What she told me blew me away: A young adult had asked her for the book *Wintergirls* by Laurie Halse Anderson, but her mother, who was with her, refused to let her teen read the book. I was intrigued and incensed that the teen had been denied access to the book she wanted to read.

I took it home and read it, fascinated and horrified by the description of a teen battling the eating disorder anorexia. I visited many libraries in Nassau County that semester, pulling together a list of books about young adults battling eating disorders, including *Nothing*, by Robin Friedman, about a teen boy battling bulimia, and *Big Fat Manifesto*, by Susan Vaught, about a teen girl with binge eating disorder. In Dr. Chelton's class, students were not allowed to just research titles and make a list. We had to actually read the books, get into the minds of the protagonists, try to empathize with their struggle, and become familiar enough with the book to be able to recommend the title in a readers' advisory scenario with a young adult patron.

When I was writing my annotations, I had in mind Dr. Chelton's lecture about bibliographic annotations. She told us that her partner and cofounder of the magazine, Dorothy Broderick, had once said that the best annotations were only one sentence long. I spent hours editing down my annotations until I had packed all the information into one interesting, informative, and grammatically correct sentence.

My bibliography was four titles long. After Dr. Chelton asked me if I would like her to submit it for publication, RoseMary Honnold got in touch with me to discuss the additional research I would need to do and the stylistic changes that I would need to make to get the piece ready for publication. She told me that I would need nonfiction sources to provide information about what eating disorders were and how they affect teens. I would also need to write in a conversational style, to make the article interesting to the readership of young adult librarians, their professors, and library science students.

So began my pursuit of information about eating disorders and young adults. I scoured the catalogs of public libraries in Nassau County and the shelves in the Rosenthal Library at Queens College. I did old-school research: I browsed the shelves and took down books with titles that seemed like they might have information I needed. I looked at the tables of contents and indexes and skimmed the pages right there in the stacks, selecting only books that had research or information that was specifically targeted to this particular topic. I downloaded e-books from Barnes and Noble on my Nook. I read everywhere: in bookstores, libraries, and classrooms and at home, taking notes and selecting quotes that I thought would work well in my article.

Once I had the hard research, I worked on finding information that would draw the reader in. I read news articles on the internet for hours, looking for just the right hook that would be interesting enough to convince someone to read until they got to the meat of the article. I did research in *Books in Print* to find out if the books I was recommending were still in print for librarians who wanted to purchase these after reading the article. Finally, I formatted my citations in Chicago, as RoseMary had instructed, to be consistent with the citation format *VOYA* required.

RoseMary added the images of the book covers and formatted the pages to look enticing and appealing. Finally, I received a check for 100 dollars and three copies of the issue where my article was published. I proudly brought them to class to show my peers and the professor.

In getting published, I knew my article would find a home in the bound books housing all of the editions of the magazine on the bottom shelf in my professor's office. Today, after Dr. Chelton's retirement, those volumes reside in the office of Dr. Anthony Bernier, who will be writing research and commentary about them for a scholarly audience. I was amazed that I had been published, before I had even graduated, in one of the most influential periodicals catering to librarians and other education professionals who serve teens.

Why am I telling this story? *VOYA*, being a resource for library professionals serving teens, was also a target at which I could aim for publication as a library school student specializing in services to children and teens. Because I had to do so much research, I also became the resident expert in the apparent symptoms of eating disorders in teens. Because I read the stories featuring fictional characters with these illnesses, I had more understanding and therefore, more empathy for young people struggling with these diseases. Five years later, I would bring to my doctor my suspicion that I, myself, had a binge eating disorder and receive treatment to cure me of that illness.

Because of *VOYA*, I wound up contributing something to the scholarly conversation about library services to young adults. This boosted my confidence and made me want to do it again, this time as a professional librarian instead of as a student. And I did. In 2013, I contributed to an article by Shari Fesko titled "Teens and Tweens After School" after securing my first professional librarian position in Mineola Memorial Library. I was hired by the director, Charles Sleefe, after working there as a page throughout library school. My Certificate in Library Service to Children and Young Adults from Queens College added a unique credential to my Master's in Library and Information Science and made me an attractive hire to this library looking to give an opportunity to a new librarian. I was hired to work in a part-time position serving adults and teens at the reference desk and children and their parents at the children's desk. The librarians were impressed with my publication in *VOYA*, and paraprofessionals in the library would often ask "Why did you do it?" I was motivated; that was why. I wanted to make a difference, like my professor had done. That was why. I wanted to prove to myself that I could take a step toward making a significant contribution. In Dr. Chelton's professional journey, I saw a path that I could follow, and I did.

At Mineola Memorial Library, I was able to plan, develop, and execute teen programs that had never been done there before. My first program was a book club, "Book and Cook," a hybrid program not in terms of technology but in terms of location. I did it in collaboration with the high school librarian at Mineola High School. We had monthly meetings. We held the first one at the public library, where we actually cooked (tacos and s'mores), then held the second one at the school library. I did a lot of reading for that program, staying on top of all the most popular and anticipated titles and collecting copies from public libraries across Nassau County to make sure they would be available for checkout by the teens attending the programs. I did a book talk about each title, just like I had been taught to do in library school, in an effort to make the titles appealing. I introduced about 12 titles at each meeting and allowed each attendee to select the book of their choice. At the next meeting, we would discuss the title they each read, and the teens would riff about the themes and topics discussed in the books. The book club and the school librarian, specifically, were formally acknowledged by the principal, who commented that the program seemed to be like a counseling session. "Yes!" I screamed in my head. That is what teens need—to be heard, to make their voices known, and to discover themselves in conversations with their peers about books with characters relevant to them.

From there, I brought to life a dream of my assistant director, Cathy Sagevick: a Tech Buddies program. I reached out to a library that was willing to share information about their teens/seniors program, which I was able to adapt

Dina Schuldner

for our library. In collaboration with Mineola High School, I recruited students, who wanted to earn volunteer credit for teaching seniors how to use their laptops, mobile phones, tablets, and even cameras. Drawing on my background in teaching seventh-graders, volunteers were taught to be respectful to seniors during their interactions and even given opportunities to test their skills on each other beforehand. They signed contracts, received sign-in sheets, and (most of them) came week after week to work with the seniors attending the library program. It was a resounding success.

After that program, I put together a teen volunteer fair at the suggestion of one of my mentors in the children's department. I started with a small directory of nonprofits that would accept teen volunteers. I wrote letters, sent emails, made phone calls, and lined up about seven agencies that agreed to come. We had a very small turnout of teens because I hadn't coordinated the event with the high school, which was doing mandatory testing that day. The following year, I expanded the fair to include adults, as my director requested. With my experience coordinating the first event, I was able to get 19 organizations to participate, and we had over 100 attendees, which was a tremendous success for our little library. I marketed the program with flyers in businesses around Mineola and using giveaways to encourage patronage at their businesses. I was told that attendees visited several of the participating businesses.

In 2013, I was hired as a part-time children's librarian at the Gold Coast Public Library. I worked both part-time jobs for about a year. After my success with teens at Mineola, I was offered the position of full-time young adult librarian at the Gold Coast Public Library.

To Gold Coast, I brought my experience from Mineola and was given the freedom to spread my wings even further. I ran summer reading for young adults for two years, bringing in teens through my outreach to the schools. I was made part of the outreach division, and my colleague and I would market library programs, find partners, and gather giveaways for the adult and young adult summer reading programs.

I had kept up with my contacts from library school. I sat down to talk with Syntychia Kendrick-Samuels, who was a very impactful young adult librarian at the Uniondale Public Library before she got promoted to assistant director. She had created an incredible program called the Teen Empowerment Academy. I wanted to do something equally impactful for the teen community of Glen Head. My efforts are documented in my third *VOYA* publication, "The Making of the Teen Entrepreneurial Academy" (2015). This program was the first of its kind offered in Nassau County and possibly, in the United States. I was asked by my director, Michael Morea, to present the program outcomes to the library's board of directors.

Fast-forward to 2023. My husband and I now reside in Virginia after his retirement from the New York Police Department. It took me five years to get back into public libraries after four years as an academic librarian. Now a branch manager, I had staff who were interested in learning how best to serve young adults. Immediately, my mind went to getting a subscription to *VOYA*. But try as I might, I could not find the website to subscribe. A couple of calls later, I discovered that the publication had ceased to exist. I could not describe the feeling of profound loss I had after hearing this. I felt as if a part of my library science education had evaporated. I felt even worse for my former professor and wondered how I would feel if the groundbreaking publication I had founded was suddenly defunct.

From my perspective, there is now an opening for a new forum that would fill the void left by *VOYA*. Dr. Chelton tells me that when it started out, the most popular section of the magazine was the review section. For me, the most important part of the magazine was the articles written by practicing young adult librarians, library workers serving young adults, and professors who were formerly young adult librarians. I had reached out to a number of these authors for more in-depth information on their topics while I was in library school.

Because of *VOYA*, I was motivated to get published. To get published, I had to do a lot of research, thereby becoming an expert in the symptoms apparent in young adults suffering with an eating disorder. Motivated to become published again, I created the groundbreaking Teen Entrepreneurial Academy at the Gold Coast Public Library, which cemented my expertise in developing programming that drew teens into the library and kept them coming back. In hindsight, I can see that *VOYA*'s mere existence had motivated me to become one of the best young adult librarians in Nassau County, which not only benefited the teens in those communities but increased the impact of the public libraries in which I worked. This raised their profile and helped secure passage of their budgets in future years.

There is an extraordinary opportunity today to develop a similar forum, where young adult librarians can share their hard-earned successes and lessons learned from trial and error in serving young adults. A well-educated and challenged young adult librarian leads to an engaged, motivated, well-rounded, and connected young adult user community. How else could we better serve our young adult communities and the profession?

DISCUSSION QUESTIONS

- What other sources of professional information can young adult librarians rely on to remain current?
- What other types of contributions can young adult librarians make to share their knowledge and experiences with colleagues?
- To what degree is YALSA (American Library Association's Young Adult Library Services Association) supporting young adult librarianship in the wake of *VOYA*'s demise?

Dina Schuldner

21

Young Adult Services in Libraries as Development Work

CONSIDER LUBUTO LIBRARY PARTNERS

Jolani Rhodenizer

Public libraries provide space and resources (print, digital, and human) to facilitate information access and foster community. This is a shared but often unscrutinized vision of libraries held by the public and library professionals. For the users loosely and variously defined as youth, this services model in practice starts from an understanding of youth as a marginalized population of near-empty information vessels in need of improvement. Public libraries that are operating in the Global South and funded as development projects frequently mirror this line of thinking. Other formal development agencies administering Western interventions in the Global South often have parallel conceptions of their beneficiaries: as people in need of services, will create movement toward some version of improvement.

However, the efficiency and efficacy of the industry of Global Northern interventions have been criticized for embodying and perpetuating neocolonial, racist, and exploitative legacies (Goldsmith, 2002; Riddel, 2014). The work done by libraries in development contexts runs this same risk. If we revise a model of young adult services independent of a definitional orientation toward "improvement," instead focusing on youth as citizens constructing their own narratives and meanings, a shift occurs. This shift allows public libraries to move toward a nuanced and complex provision of youth services, a change especially necessary in development contexts. Lubuto Library Partners operating in Zambia provides a reenvisioned framework of how to design, implement, and manage a transformational, collaborative young adult services model that can be called *development librarianship*.

MODELS OF YOUNG ADULT SERVICES IN LIBRARY AND INFORMATION SCIENCE

Youth Services in library and information science (LIS) has been criticized as being rooted in an industrial age that is now over, neglectful of its obligation to adapt and reflect changing cultural, social, and economic obligations as a publicly accountable institution (Bernier, 2020). This model envisions youth as objects, unrealized, pre-adult empty vessels expected to complete a prescribed trajectory toward a predefined version of acceptable adults. Such ideas are frequently laden with sociocultural, racial, colonial, heteronormative, and gendered prescriptions, which often privilege white forms of knowing and understanding (Kumasi, 2020). Unfortunately, to understand a group of library users in this disempowered way leads to a failure to design service models that are cognizant of "what it is to be a young adult at this point in time and in the complex of society" (Budd, 2020, p. 10).

Contrasting with a youth-as-object is a model of LIS that identifies these users as fully realized subjects engaging from and within the present society, where childhood and youth are ends in themselves. As Kozol (2005) popularly put it, "childhood is not merely basic training for utilitarian adulthood. It should have some claims upon our mercy, not for its future value to the economic interests of competitive societies but for its present value as a perishable piece of life itself" (p. 2). Conceptualizations and categorizations of youth are contested and often rely on stereotypes that are moralizing or biologically based (Rothbauer, 2020). Applying the discourse of critical youth studies (Kelly & Kamp, 2015) allows us to move away from biological constructions of youth and toward one that is socially constructed and dynamic. This avoids the competing ideologies around the period of youth as either precious or tabula rasa (Rothbauer, 2020).

Shifting toward conceptualizations of youth as fully realized humans speaking from a subjective location that is individualized, contextualized, and self-evidently valuable, places young adults as reflective agents in their own lives, not objects of professional services (Budd, 2020). As Bernier (2020) puts it, "the question thus shifts from *if* youth have power to asking *how* their power is defined, negotiated, navigated, exercised, documented, manifested, and recognized" (p. 178).

LIBRARIES AND DEVELOPMENT

Public libraries in development contexts operate at the intersection of the legacies of young adult services and Western interventions in the Global South. The dominant notion within development efforts of a linear progression toward positive change achieved by the movement of funding, labor, and good intentions is reflective of a colonial legacy of economic exploitation and white saviorism (Goldsmith, 2002). Generally, the development intention is to create or increase well-being, enhancing the "capacity of economic, political and social systems to provide the circumstances for that well-being on a sustainable, long-term basis" (Barder, 2012). Collectively, these initiatives have long been critiqued for the lack of local engagement in the planning and execution of initiatives, instead aligning with an externally defined notion of what development is and ought to be (Riddel, 2014).

Libraries and LIS have not managed to escape this neocolonial trap. A well-known example is the plethora of Global North to South literacy and library programs whose ill-conceived purpose is to donate used books to "poor African children." Narrowly conceptualizing development librarianship as getting books in the hands of "underprivileged youth" is problematic and ill thought through in terms of the on-the-ground resources necessary to make this happen (Lor, 2019).

Youth development work and youth services ought not to be the same thing. While often overlapping, LIS does not necessarily need to understand itself as intentional, as part of the "youth development industrial complex (YDIC)" (Bernier, 2020). The intentionality of achieving specific outcomes creates a patronizing organizational purpose, an assumption that youth need to be different than they are in identified and measurable ways and libraries have a social responsibility to make that happen (Chelton, 2020).

To overcome this, reflexive consultation between libraries, community leadership, and political authorities is necessary, both locally and nationally. Unscrutinized good intentions are likely to result in uniform understandings of what is needed and what is possible as well as missed opportunities to gain access to promising pathways to buy-in and collaboration (Lor, 2019). Public libraries can function as agents in the pursuit of development outcomes by providing access and services necessary for the creation and enhancement of literacy and employability skills that are necessary to thrive. However, a responsive services model where youth can access library resources as creators and agents, fulfilling their own agendas to increase choice and capabilities, does not assume a responsibility for public libraries to move youth along a continuum of improvement. It creates space for this change but does not prioritize it the way it has been in the legacies of youth services and development work.

THE LUBUTO LIBRARY MODEL

One organization that is challenging the confluence of hegemonic development models and young adult services with an innovative transdisciplinary operational model is Lubuto Library Partners (http://www.lubuto.org/). Operating in Zambia since 2005, Lubuto values youth as "users who are defined by their already existing position in the world as young adults . . . in ways that are wholly appropriate to that position" (Rothbauer, 2020, p. 171). In practice, this means bridging gaps in services and forming connections between development agencies and public libraries as collaborative partners. Lubuto has transformational intentions, having "successfully pioneered the use of public libraries as a platform for cross-sectoral impact and challenged narrow perceptions about what a library can be and do" (Lubuto, 2019, para. 2).

The Lubuto model is based on reciprocal learning through truly collaborative planning and evaluation processes that embrace stakeholders at all levels, including most importantly, young people. By utilizing praxis from both the fields of LIS and development, Lubuto can successfully provide multilaterally managed, locally responsive services embedded in Zambia's peoples and histories.

The Lubuto model engages with youth as subjects experiencing their own lives in the present, lives that manifest as freestanding modes of existence.

Aligning with the UN Sustainable Development Goals metric (Cramer, 2017; Mukonde, 2017), Lubuto has been widely recognized with financial support and partnerships throughout its history, including USAID and the Open Society Initiative of Southern Africa (OSISA).

What makes Lubuto transdisciplinary and innovative is not only its organizational model. A foundational component of its services is the collection development policy, which is centered on the "ongoing identification of excellent, relevant and accessible youth literature from around the world to provide balanced library collections that meet evolving needs and interests, along with all historical and current materials written by or about Zambians both as an accessible repository and, when possible, a print collection in each Lubuto library" (J. Meyers, personal communication, April 30, 2023). Additionally, Lubuto has ongoing programming in areas such as health, education, psychosocial support, technology, arts, and culture, conscientiously developed in response to the needs, priorities, and interests of the communities served and sustained through local partnerships. In addition to literacy-focused programming, they offer mentorship and scholarship programs targeting the very salient issue of reduction of early marriage for girls. They host makerspaces where girls can learn skills, such as sewing or pottery, that are both marketable and pleasurable (for a complete listing of model programs, see https://www.lubuto.org/programs). This collusion of the dual expectations of services, which permit time and space for creative expression, personal growth, and exploration, while simultaneously providing opportunities toward the creation of economic advantage, is distinctly development librarianship, derived from the lives of users and their communities. It is an emergent model of LIS, one that understands development as an equal but not singular priority. It is conceptualized as a collaborative, transdisciplinary young adult services model rooted in the present, with an eye on the future and always listening.

RECOMMENDATIONS

Libraries are currently not thought of as development partners by nongovernmental organizations (NGOs) (Lynch et al., 2020). This may partly be due to the insistence of LIS to unreflexively cling to legacy self-conceptions of youth services as solely in the domain of literacy learning. However, public libraries are doing development work. This points to the potential for a new focus area in LIS educational programs and the creation of development librarianship as a career pathway. Some LIS education programs are attempting to address this in their coursework, aiming to provide opportunities for learners to develop an appreciation of their profession as situated within a global environment with diverse conceptions of intellectual freedom and information literacy (Hirsh et al., 2015). It may take time until this creeps into praxis. However, in the meantime, LIS programs and professionals can look to notable exceptions such as Lubuto as models for effective, locally embedded, and responsive provision of young adult services in development contexts.

DISCUSSION QUESTIONS

*   How does Lubuto's model of young adult services differ from conventional young adult services in the United States?
*   What obstacles and opportunities might exist for a library attempting to more closely implement Lubuto's model in the United States?
*   What service components offered by Lubuto could be used to enhance young adult services in the United States?
*   What challenges for implementing service components like Lubuto's into the United States might you anticipate? What resources might be helpful in addressing them?
*   What specific information sources would you seek to learn more about international models of library services?

REFERENCES

Barder, O. (2012, August 16). *What is development?* [Blog post]. Center for Global Development. https://www.cgdev.org/blog/what-development.

Bernier, A. (2020). Moving beyond YAs as "citizens": The promise of membership. *Transforming young adult services* (2nd ed., pp. 173–88). ALA-Neal Schuman.

Budd, J. (2020). Foreword. In A. Bernier (Ed.), *Transforming young adult services* (2nd ed.). (pp. 9–11). ALA Neal-Schuman.

Chelton, M. (2020). LIS's vision of young adults: Some historical roots for current theories and practice. In A. Bernier (Ed.), *Transforming young adult services* (2nd ed., pp. 145–51). ALA Neal-Schuman.

Cramer, E. (2017). Partnering in international library development: Lubuto library partners, Zambia library service, and Zambia's ministry of education. In C. Constantinou,

M. Miller, & K. Schlesinger (Eds.), *International librarianship: Developing professional, intercultural, and educational leadership* (pp. 131–43). State University of New York Press.

Goldsmith, E. (2002). Development as colonialism. *World Affairs: The Journal of International Issues, 6*(2), 18–36. http://www.jstor.org/stable/45064890.

Hirsh, S., Simmons, M. H., Christensen, P., Sellar, M., Stenström, C., Hagar, C., Bernier, A., Faires, D., Fisher, J., & Alman, S. (2015). International perspectives in LIS education: Global education, research, and collaboration at the SJSU school of information. *Journal of Education for Library and Information Science, 56*(S1), S27–S46. https://www.jstor.org/stable/90015099.

Kelly, P., & Kamp, A. (2015). *A critical youth studies for the 21st century.* Brill.

Kozol, J. (2005). Preparing minds for markets. *School Administrator, 62*(9), 31–34.

Kumasi, K. (2020). The library is like her house. In A. Bernier (Ed.), *Transforming young adult services* (2nd ed). (pp. 132–37). ALA Neal-Schuman.

Lor, P. (2019, September 26). *Libraries and systemic development work* [Blog post]. https://peterlor.com/2019/09/26/libraries-and-systemic-development-work/.

Lubuto Library Partners. (2019). *Libraries transforming Africa's next generation.* https://static1.squarespace.com/static/557edb36e4b0c3993dee95d1/t/5d8cfa910b0e79221d611411/1569520276254/2019+Handout.pdf.

Lynch, R., Young, J. C., Jowaisas, C., Boakye-Achampong, S., & Sam, J. (2020). African libraries in development: Perceptions and possibilities. *The International Information & Library Review, 53*(4), 277–90. https://doi.org/10.1080/10572317.2020.1840002.

Mukonde, K. T. (2017, May 7). *Lubuto Libraries in Zambia: Sustainable development through library and information services* [Paper presented]. IFLA WLIC 2017, Poland. http://library.ifla.org/id/eprint/1695/1/139-mukonde-en.pdf.

Riddell, R. (2014, February 13). *Does foreign aid really work?* [Paper presented]. Australasian Aid and International Development Workshop, Canberra. http://devpolicy.org/2014-Australasian-Aid-and-International-Development-Policy-Workshop/Papers/Keynotes/Roger-Riddell-Keynote-Address.pdf.

Rothbauer, P. (2020). Imagining today's young adults in LIS moving forward with critical youth studies. In A. Bernier (Ed.), *Transforming young adult services* (2nd ed., pp. 163–72). ALA Neal-Schuman.

22

Organizing a Young Adult Services Unit

VERTICAL OR HORIZONTAL INTEGRATION

Anthony Bernier

INTRODUCTION

Providing public value to audiences of young adults today remains a constant challenge for libraries, as it has throughout library history, whether the challenges come in the form of economic cutbacks, staff shortages, or resource inequities or in staff attitudes, political disputes, or public health crises. Sometimes libraries can address these challenges quickly using available resources. At other times, challenges require more long-term strategic thinking.

Among the more strategic opportunities that libraries can exploit to address ongoing challenges in delivering quality young adult services is to study, adopt, and implement an overarching model of services delivery.

I have developed two different organizational models that offer respective opportunities. The first model is likely more traditionally recognized: "vertical integration." A vertically integrated model of young adult services seeks to specialize and separate young adult services from other library units—envisioning young adults as inhabiting a particular, specific, and different moment in their growth into adulthood.

The second model, "horizontal integration," conversely, focuses on young adults more intergenerationally as active contributors throughout the library's entire public services profile, concentrating on what young adults *share* with other user groups, not simply what differentiates them.

The following essay characterizes the essential details in each of these two organizational models as well as offers a comparative analysis between these different ways in which to strategize, organize, and implement young adult services. While each of these models is rendered here as an ideal type, both can be combined in different formations. But it is helpful for library professionals to be aware of their unique opportunities as well as their respective challenges.

VERTICAL INTEGRATION

Today's libraries organize and deliver young adult services in a variety of ways. However, among the most common approaches remains a "silo" model in which young adult services cordon off, specialize, and vertically integrate into age-segregated services, the way libraries traditionally separate services for children and adults.

Libraries enact this model assuming it better focuses age-specific professional and institutional capacities on the particular needs of young adult audiences and users. Libraries view children's services, too, as delivered better by children's specialists based on their deeper understanding of children's resources and institutional capacities and the informational world of children. Likewise, adult services specialist librarians command broad professional knowledge, skills, and resources required of that user population.

Organized this way, libraries execute collections, plan and evaluate programs, interpret library policy and ethical standards, and focus supervision of library support staff to serve specific age categories of users. In a vertically integrated organizational model, responsibilities between units do not overlap much.

OPPORTUNITIES FOR VERTICALLY INTEGRATED YOUNG ADULT SERVICES

A vertically integrated young adult services organizational model delivers library services and benefits through professional expertise by segregating the young adult user community. In a vertically integrated unit, the specifics of young adult experience define a library's young adult service profile. Young adult programming, for example, involves only young adults and young adult–related topics. The young adult specialist librarian recruits and supervises young adult volunteers. Teen advisory groups (TAGs) and boards consist of only young adults and focus attention on matters of young adult programming, collections, technology, events, spaces, exhibits, and so on. Outreach efforts include only young adult institutions executed by young adult staff. Vertically integrated young adult services measure and report on young adult library services outputs (such as the number of young adult programs and attendees) and outcomes (things young adult users report having changed as a result of library services).

Vertically integrated young adult services also offer librarians the opportunity to focus their training and professional development on serving a demographic group widely recognized as having particular needs different from children and adults. Vertical integration delineates clear lines of expertise, authority, responsibility, accountability, and institutional influence. In other words, a young adult librarian can usually count on asserting greater influence on library policy pertaining to young adult services than adult librarians.

Vertical integration of young adult services also potentially supports advocacy for and protection of library resource allocation. A young adult specialist librarian would work to ensure that young adult services receives an equitable and proportionate share of library resources because they represent needs distinct from other service populations.

Vertically integrated young adult services, however, would generally not include adult librarians involved with young adult programs, collections, events, spaces, exhibits, outreach, and so on. Adult librarians would not be expected to track and report on young adult services metrics. Nor would the service components of adult or children's services be commonly considered of interest to young adult audiences or marketed or promoted to them.

Vertical integration remains the more traditional organizational model for libraries and thus, is more culturally sanctioned within the library community.

EXAMPLES OF VERTICALLY INTEGRATED YOUNG ADULT SERVICES

As the vertically integrated model of young adult services remains the more familiar and practiced approach, it focuses exclusively on work with young adults. Libraries direct all young adult resources toward young adult–specific experience as administered by young adult staff. Young adult staff would be responsible for reporting to library administration on young adult activity.

Vertically integrated young adult programming, for instance, would engage topics and content targeted specifically for young adult interests and young adult–specific audiences. Programming ideas might come from surveying young adult users and focus groups, professional young adult media, or conventional associational sources such as regional groups of young adult librarians or YALSA's "Calendar of Teen Programming Ideas." Young adult programming organized vertically would be planned and administered largely through a young adult services department and young adult staff. Programming would be scheduled to accommodate school and vacation calendars. Promotional efforts would conventionally focus on attracting young adult audiences from schools or other local youth-serving organizations.

A vertically integrated teen advisory group (TAG) represents another example. Organized vertically, a TAG might meet periodically or regularly with young adult staff and discuss favorite young adult books, magazines, films, and authors. A vertically integrated TAG might develop young adult programming ideas and even help promote them to young adult audiences. Such a TAG might produce a newsletter or publish a blog on the library's website about young adult services and activities.

Vertically integrated young adult services would be the responsibility of library young adult staff. Young adult participation and involvement would focus on and within the young adult services unit. Young adult staff would not generally be responsible for working closely with other library units that do not pertain directly to young adult services. On staff training days, the young adult library staff might deliver a workshop on young adult services.

CHALLENGES FOR VERTICALLY INTEGRATED YOUNG ADULT SERVICES

While several institutional advantages accrue to young adult services organized with a vertically integrated model, and there is nothing inherently "wrong" or bad in organizing services this way, still, possible challenges and drawbacks do present themselves. Among the challenges attending the vertically integrated young adult services model is that few library professionals are trained to work specifically with young adults—compared with the number of children's specialists. Most "youth librarians" receive training to serve children, and thus, it can be difficult to implement an entire organizational model based on the age segregation required in serving young adults.

A second challenge presented by vertical integration is that the institutionally constructed age-based segregation of young adults from other service units inherently emphasizes only the *differences* between young adults and the other demographic categories (children and especially, adults). In these instances, young adults interested in children's programs, for instance, or "adult" events, such as an author talk, would be excluded or feel unwelcome. These distinctions rather inhibit young adult user agency, choice, and self-selection, which can contradict a library's mission to offer access to the library's resources to everyone.

Vertical integration can also perpetuate other unintended consequences. Because young adults have long been perceived as a problematic population in libraries, segregating young adult services can paper over these perceptions and attitudes rather than address them. If other staff know that "the young adult librarian is in charge of the young adults," then there is no motivation or accountability for the rest of the library to improve the library's overall public services profile with young people.

Ultimately, in organizing young adult services vertically, as a self-contained unit within the library, the institution inherently sanctions a particular vision and definition of young adults. That is, young adults are defined only, exclusively, and inherently as a separate group. Young adult services organized this way also envisions young adults largely as consumers of library services and program offerings.

Thus, young adult *difference* from other groups remains the institutionalized focus. Engagement in the nature and scope of young adult involvement, participation, and contributions remains predetermined, permanent, limited,

Anthony Bernier

and segregated rather arbitrarily by age rather than interests, varying levels of maturity, skills, or even curiosity. The institution would rarely, if ever, confront entrenched institutional inequities in resources or attitudes.

Taken as a whole, while vertically integrated young adult services can benefit from specialization, it can also hamper the library from connecting service outputs and outcomes to broad library mission, vision, and aspirations.

HORIZONTAL INTEGRATION

While not sacrificing a young adult specialist's professional efficacy or expertise, a library can elect to implement an alternative I have articulated in contrast to the traditional vertical integration model of young adult services. The alternative, *horizontal* integration, offers libraries a vision of young adults less as an exclusively different user group than active agents and contributing members within *the broader library community in addition to* being services consumers.

Simply put, rather than containing all young adult services components and experiences within an age-segregated model, a horizontally integrated model assembles and delivers services so that *young adults play roles in all parts of the library* as a complex public services organization. As with the vertical integration model, however, there are opportunities as well as potential challenges.

OPPORTUNITIES FOR HORIZONTALLY INTEGRATED YOUNG ADULT SERVICES

A horizontally integrated model offers many potential opportunities for proving a rich and dynamic young adult services profile. First, horizontal integration offers the library a more progressive and broader opportunity to envision young adults themselves. Beyond viewing young adults traditionally as needy, lacking skills, or pre- or sub-adults (focused entirely on young adult differences from adults), a horizontally integrated young adult unit envisions them as capable, caring, and contributing members to the library and its community in ways that focus more on what young adults *share and have in common with others in the here and now.* Second, a horizontally integrated model offers opportunities for professional library staff, who may lack specific young adult training to nevertheless develop a strong service response. Because this vision of young adults seeks to incorporate young people into the library as a civic institution, it avoids pigeonholing, predetermining, and delimiting young adult experience and meaning. And professional staff facilitating stronger ties with other units would be seen as contributing more directly to the library's broad vision and mission than merely reporting young adult–specific output measures such as summer reading program sign-ups. Horizontally integrated young adult services implicitly advocates for and identifies ways in which young adults are seen and heard and contribute across the library's entire institutional footprint.

Another opportunity in horizontal integration is how it institutionalizes intergenerational mixing. Rather than partitioning young adults into a narrow age-based category, horizontal integration seeks ways young adults can join and actively participate with other caring library community members and supporters. It introduces young adults to the more "adult" world as productive agents, while also enhancing the profile and reputation of young people as contributing members of the library community and the public. Thus, this model contributes to building young adult social capital and confidence in the broader public world. It widens young adult capacities for appreciating the entire public services value of the library. It heightens their regard for the library as a public institution within the wider civic community.

Finally, and in stark contrast to vertical integration, horizontal integration of young adult services also benefits the entire institution—highlighting the contributions of young adults in their various roles as contributing members of the library community to staff, administration, library support groups, and policy makers.

The horizontal integration and involvement of young adults across the entire library services profile, in varying roles and at appropriate levels of intensity, better ensures their higher degree of knowledge about library affairs. And higher levels of institutional knowledge inform greater confidence for library advocacy.

EXAMPLES OF HORIZONTALLY INTEGRATED YOUNG ADULT SERVICES

The horizontal integration of young adult services envisions young people not simply within a demographic age category but as fully entitled and participatory community members contributing throughout the entire institution. With this organizational model, young adult programs, for instance, actively welcome not only young adults but everyone in the community as audience members—friends, family, teachers, library staff, and media as well as other members of the library support community. In this way, also, the age-old fear of "nobody showing up for a young adult program" declines tremendously.

Organized horizontally, library staff would not select or deliver program content. Here, young people themselves, not adults, come forward from the community to perform, display, curate, or exhibit *their* interests and experiences before the entire library community. In a horizontally integrated young adult services unit, young adults become the subjects *and* content providers—thus avoiding the traditional treatment of young adults as the objects or mere consumers of young adult–specific content delivered by adults.

Conversely, a horizontally integrated young adult services unit offers young people participatory roles in "adult" programming as well. Prepared young adults serve as event ushers, help staff the library information table, attend the pre- or post-author reception, and take photos with and receive author-signed books. Libraries would also encourage young adults to serve on event panels with adults or deliver informed young adult perspectives at library foundation meetings.

Anthony Bernier

Beyond programming, however, horizontal integration also expands the scope, reach, and imagination of what a TAG can achieve. A horizontally integrated TAG incorporates proportionate young adult exposures to all library operations: various administrative functions (such as conducting short informational interviews with personnel sampled from across all library operations and perhaps other civic institutions), receiving budget briefings, and learning about political and personnel processes. Young adults might play roles in staff development events—delivered either in live or recorded presentations. An active and informed TAG might participate in library advocacy through helping with a library bond campaign and representing youth at state legislative day.

An experienced TAG might also contribute the "young adult voice" to a library's facilities planning process. They would make informed contributions about the design of facilities and library spaces (not only the young adult space). They might participate in or observe meetings with architects and planners. While, of course, excused from confidential legal aspects of the process, young adults might participate in contractor selection discussions along with the adult public or staff.

At base, the horizontally integrated young adult services model *actively* seeks meaningful exposure, observation, and participatory roles for young people across the *entire institution*, not just in young adult services. The same organizational agenda would be pursued for all aspects of library services: TAGs, volunteer roles, collection development, outreach activities, staff training, policy and space planning, and service evaluation.

CHALLENGES FOR HORIZONTALLY INTEGRATED YOUNG ADULT SERVICES

Of course, focusing more sophisticated attention on this age demographic can alone present challenges in innovating away from the traditional age-segregated services model. Library professionals, for instance, to the degree they studied youth services in library school, likely were introduced to traditional approaches to young adult services. Most youth courses include a strong curricular bias for books and literature (chiefly fiction) that risk inadequately and more comprehensively covering other aspects of library services such as program development and evaluation, just to name two. Such a circumstance leaves little room to imagine young adults as participating and contributing broadly in the library's broader public affairs profile.

Second, young adult services are traditionally not well supported with evidence-based research. Consequently, library school students would likely encounter a long-lingering and highly dated vision of young adults rooted in the nineteenth-century notion of "youth development." This theoretical approach to young people envisions them as ever and only differentiated from so-called mature adults. Further, the youth development theory, among other negative features, imagines young adults only as works in progress, skill deficient, and

Service Components	Vertically Integrated Model	Horizontally Integrated Model
Events (readings, author visits, celebrations, etc...)	YA events only	YAs involved in all events
Programs (clubs, workshops, classes)	YA content only	YAs involved in all programs
Collection Development	YA input in YA collections	YAs exposed to all collection development
Volunteer Opportunities	YAs volunteer in YA service unit (perhaps children's unit)	YAs volunteer in all library units
Teen Advisory Group (TAG)/YA Advisory Boards (TAB)	Focus on YA services	Connected to, exposed to, learning about all library operations
Staff Training	YA staff train on YA services	YA staff train all library staff about YA involvement and contributions to library at all levels
Policy	YA staff concerned with YA service policy	YA staff facilitate YA exposure to, and involvement in, all library policy
Library governance	YA staff aware of library governance pertaining to YA services	YA staff facilitate exposure to, and involvement in, all library governance
Space	YA staff focused on YA space	YA staff facilitate YA exposure to, and involvement in, all library facilities
Tutoring	YA staff manage or supervise YA tutoring	YA serve as 'tutors' for things they excel at
Outreach	YA staff conduct outreach efforts with YA involved institutions (mostly schools)	YA staff facilitate YA exposure to, and involvement in, all library outreach efforts
Evaluation of Programs & Services	YA staff evaluate YA services programs	YAs participate in evaluating all library services and programs
Administration functions (budget, personnel, facilities, etc.)	No role for YAs	YA staff facilitate appropriate YA exposure to all administration functions
Building social capital	YAs meet other YAs	YAs meet and participate with other adults and staff

Figure 22.1. Comparing Vertical and Horizontal Integration

in preparation for some idealized, fully actuated, future "adulthood." In other words, the youth development theory offers little for an age-integrated approach valuing young adult experience in the present and how they can *share* certain experiences with adults in the public world.

Finally, given library tradition, it can be challenging for library staff to consider or accept young adults' participation across the organization's entire profile. Doing so runs counter to separating user groups demographically by age. It can contradict organizational culture and appear to challenge conventional lines of responsibility and authority. Consequently, the model of horizontal integration viewing young adults as actively contributing members of the larger library community may challenge young adult staff to expand young adult involvement through creating participatory roles in traditionally adult-only activities and organizations (such as friends of the library, the library commission, the library board, and amity-based organizations).

CONCLUSION

While the best way to organize a library's young adult services unit depends on a library's particular resources and organizational culture, the way in which a library envisions its young adult population will influence the degree to which the young adult services is vertically or horizontally integrated. Different organizational models for delivering young adult services each presents respective challenges and opportunities. Circumstances such as staff capacities, expertise, local community needs, and different library visions of the young adult population also substantially influence the degree to which one model is pursued or how a library might selectively "borrow" from or combine features from one model or the other, or transition from one model to another. And transitioning from one model to another would require thoughtful strategic planning over time and necessarily involve library-wide discussion.

Thus, I have created these ideal model types to acknowledge different orientations of young adult staff expertise and specialization. Both models can achieve excellence for young adults in terms of engaging services and participatory roles. Either model advances the library as a civic institution delivering quality public value in promoting the building of individual and collective social capital and access to library resources.

DISCUSSION QUESTIONS

- What factors are most important in implementing each of these two service models?
- What steps would you take to involve young adults in choosing one model over the other?

REFERENCE

YALSA. (n.d.). *Calendar of teen programming ideas.* https://wikis.ala.org/yalsa/index.php
/Calendar_of_Teen_Programming_Ideas.

Anthony Bernier

23

Learning about Race, Racism, and Whiteness in School Library Preparation Programs

Julia Burns Petrella

Imagine a high school library. How big is it? Does it span more than one room? What kind of lighting is in the space and what type of shelving? Are there tables for students to work in groups? What about couches or comfortable armchairs? Does the library have computers or other technology for students to use? How does the circulation area where students can check out materials look? Once you have this imagined library in your mind, picture the school librarian. What are they wearing? Where are they located in the library, and what are they doing? Do they look friendly and welcoming?

Are you imagining a white woman? It would not be surprising if you are because it is well documented that librarianship is an overwhelmingly white[1] profession (Cooke et al., 2017; Honma, 2005; Hughes-Hassell & Vance, 2015; Pawley, 2006). According to a study of demographics of more than 37,500 members of the American Library Association, 86.7 percent of the respondents self-identified as white (Rosa & Henke, 2017). The numbers only get whiter when we look at school librarians more specifically: The 2012 ALA Diversity Counts report showed that 90.3 percent of school librarians reported their race to be white. With statistics such as these, it is not an understatement to say that a lack of racial diversity exists in librarianship.

In contrast, the racial demographics of students in elementary and secondary schools in the United States have been trending steadily away from a white majority, with white students making up only 45.2 percent of the national student body in 2021 (National Center for Education Statistics, 2021). The table below illustrates this demographic distinction between students and school librarians.

This demographic disparity has been termed the *diversity gap* by Putman et al. (2016), which specifically refers to "the difference in the proportion of minority teachers and minority students in public schools" (p. 2) that has had a significant effect on student experience and learning. In their research on white educators working with students of color, Miller and Harris (2018) describe what they call *symptoms of whiteness*, which includes "colorblind ideology, a false sense of equality, deficits-based thinking, lowered academic expectations, white messiah syndrome or white saviority, and superficial multicultural education" (p. 2). The diversity gap between school librarians and our nation's students, as well as determinants, such as the symptoms of whiteness described above, highlight how important it is that school librarians in training are knowledgeable about race, racism, and whiteness. So what factors affect how preservice school librarians learn about these topics in their school library preparation programs?

In seeking an answer to this question, I interviewed 11 school librarianship students and 5 recent graduates of school library preparation programs. Among this group of 16 participants, 11 (68.7 percent) self-identified as white, and 5 (31.3 percent) self-identified as nonwhite, reporting their races in the following ways: Black American, Half-Japanese, Latino/a, Mexican American,

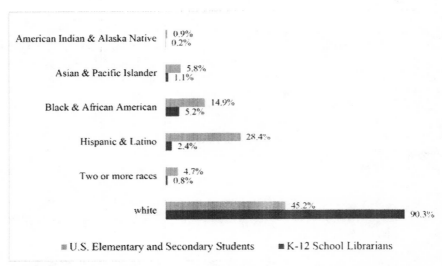

Table 23.1. Racial Demographics of Elementary/Secondary Students and K-12 School Librarians

Julia Burns Petrella

and Taiwanese American. The participant names used in this chapter are gender-neutral pseudonyms.

The participants in this study identified several factors that influenced their learning about topics of race, racism, and whiteness, including the impact of specific instructors, the impact of racial diversity within the classroom, and the impact of personal interest and initiative.

THE IMPACT OF INDIVIDUAL INSTRUCTORS

The students and graduates pointed to the impact of individual instructors as a significant factor in their overall exposure to topics of race, racism, and whiteness in the school library programs. August, a white student, identified a specific instructor who "always, always, always emphasized diversity," while Kai, a white 2019 graduate, described an instructor who "talked about race and racism regularly. And sort of like it was a part of our professional life to have to combat racism."

Dana, a Taiwanese American student, said that there were two instructors in particular that they sought out based on the types of courses they taught or rumors that the instructor centered topics of social justice more so than other instructors. Dana said:

> I happened upon [instructor A]'s classes, which are electives . . . and I was very fortunate I had heard [instructor B]'s class was more social justice focused, which is why I took it instead of taking it with other professors. If I hadn't taken [instructor A]'s class, and if I hadn't taken [instructor B]'s class, I don't think I had would have had this deep dive [into topics of race], and I wouldn't have come on to these type of projects. . . . It wouldn't have been this deep and it wouldn't have been as meaningful and impactful.

THE IMPACT OF DIVERSITY IN THE CLASSROOM

The participants shared their insights on the impact that racial diversity in the classroom—or the lack thereof—had on their experiences of learning about race, racism, and whiteness. A handful of participants remarked on how they imagined their experience of learning about race, racism, and whiteness would have been improved in their library and information science (LIS) program with more racial diversity among the instructors (Jamie, white 2021 graduate; Kris, white student; Sam, white 2018 graduate). Indeed, participants shared that having instructors of color created a class environment that facilitated more productive conversations about topics of race, racism, and whiteness. Kai, a white 2019 graduate said:

> I think like I mentioned [instructor name] being one of the few Black profes- sors I had. . . . There was a difference between how she facilitated and how

white folks facilitated. . . . It just seems like they're more matter of fact, and like, this is what is happening, rather than holding our hand or babying people. It's just like, you know, there's no pretending. You gotta, like, talk about it. . . . That seems pretty important for this work.

Likewise, Whit, a Mexican American student, explained that courses taught by nonwhite instructors allowed for deeper, more frequent conversations about race.

Whit: "I can honestly say that I really enjoyed doing a deep dive into racial categories and that sort of thing. So, my classes that were taught by my minority teachers . . . when you have people that are in the same situation, it's a little bit easier to talk about."

Julia (interviewer): "So, you found that [in] the classes where you had minority instructors, those conversations about race were happening at a deeper level or more often?"

Whit: "Deeper *and* more often. Yes."

THE IMPACT OF PERSONAL INTEREST AND INITIATIVE

Some of the students and graduates described ways that they took personal initiative to learn more about topics of race, racism, or whiteness in their programs. When the participants shared their memories of assignments, discussions, and readings that were related to topics of race, racism, or whiteness, a few specified that they were given the freedom to include or explore these topics, though they were not specifically assigned. August, a white student, recalled that students had the option to focus on diversity when completing a lesson plan assignment, saying: "I don't think it was required to do a lesson plan that involved diversity, but it was made available." Similarly, Dana, a Taiwanese American student, reported that when they were given a choice of assigned readings, they "gravitated towards" topics relating to race.

Another way that participants took initiative to learn about race, racism, or whiteness was by choosing to take elective courses that centered on these topics, which were often otherwise missing from the school librarianship curriculum. Jordan, a white student, explained: "In taking [the elective course], I kind of brought opportunities in for myself that wouldn't have been part of the school librarianship track."

Some also described ways that they personally brought up topics of race, racism, or whiteness when they felt that it was not being covered sufficiently by their courses. Kris, a white student, described advocating for more focus on topics relating to race, racism, and whiteness in the school library preparation program by contacting the school library program coordinator at their institution. Corey, a Latino/a student, said, "I took a [school library specific] course . . . and we didn't specifically talk about race, but I always tried to bring it up since it was a very white—it was like a white centered [course]." As a follow-up question during the interview, I asked Corey how it felt to bring up topics of race when it wasn't otherwise being discussed in class. Corey replied, "Sometimes it's intimidating, but I feel like my intimidation isn't as important, or the anxiety that I feel isn't as important, as the topic that needs to be broached. So like at the end of the day, after I've done it, I usually don't mind."

In summary, a handful of factors affect how preservice school librarians are exposed to topics of race, racism, and whiteness in their school library preparation programs, including the impact of specific instructors, the impact of diversity in the classroom, and the impact of personal interest and initiative. So what lessons can we take from this? Here are a few of my personal takeaways from this study:

- Hone your personal interest in topics relating to race, racism, and whiteness. Read and learn widely about the effects of whiteness and the ways that all of us are consciously and unconsciously bound up in it. Reflect deeply on your own race and the ways that your race could affect your work as a librarian.
- Seek out courses and instructors that focus specifically on these issues. Spotlight these topics in your assignments and class discussions. Share your knowledge with others through class presentations; conference talks; and conversations with other students, colleagues, and instructors.
- Advocate for the inclusion of discussions and readings on the ways that concepts relating to race intertwine with librarianship. Speak out when discussions of these topics remain superficial or insincere.

DISCUSSION QUESTIONS

- What are some topics relating to race and racism that you feel should be included in school library programs? Do any of these have implications for serving youth?
- What steps can new professional librarians introduce into productive discussions about whiteness among colleagues?
- What young adult services policies require revising upon acknowledging the implications of whiteness?

NOTE

1. The term *white* is lowercased throughout this document following the lead of Corces-Zimmerman and Guida (2019), who deliberately lowercase this word to "challenge hegemonic grammatical norms" and to remove power given to the concept through capitalizing it (p. 92).

REFERENCES

ALA Diversity Counts. (2012). *Table Series A: 2009-2010 American Community Survey Estimates Applied to Institute for Museum and Library Services and National Center for Education Statistics Data American Library Association (ALA)*. American Library Association. http://www.ala.org/aboutala/sites/ala.org.aboutala/files/content/diversity/diversitycounts/diversitycountstables2012.pdf

Cooke, N. A., Spencer, K., Jacobs, J. M., Mabbott, C., Collins, C., & Loyd, R. M. (2017). Mapping topographies from the classroom: Addressing whiteness in the LIS curriculum. In G. Schlesselman-Tarango (Ed.), *Topographies of whiteness: Mapping whiteness in library and information science* (pp. 235-50). Library Juice Press.

Corces-Zimmerman, C., & Guida, T. F. (2019). Toward a critical whiteness methodology: Challenging whiteness through qualitative research. In J. Huisman and M. Tight (Eds.), *Theory and method in higher education research* (Vol. 5, pp. 91-109). Emerald Publishing Limited.

Honma, T. (2005). Trippin' over the color line: The invisibility of race in library and information studies. *InterActions: UCLA Journal of Education and Information Studies, 1*(2).

Hughes-Hassell, S., & Vance, K. J. (2015). Examining race, power, privilege and equity in the youth services LIS classroom. In N. A. Cooke and M. E. Sweeney (Eds.), *Teaching for justice: Implementing social justice in the LIS classroom* (pp. 103-38). Litwin Books/Library Juice Press.

Miller, L. A., & Harris, V. W. (2018). I can't be racist—I teach in an urban school, and I'm a nice white lady! *World Journal of Education, 8*(3), 1-11.

National Center for Education Statistics. (2021). *Table 216.50. Number and percentage distribution of public elementary and secondary school students, by percentage of minority enrollment in the school and student's racial/ethnic group: Selected years, fall 1995 through fall 2019*. https://nces.ed.gov/programs/digest/d21/tables/dt21_216.50.asp.

Pawley, C. C. (2006). Unequal legacies: Race and multiculturalism in the LIS curriculum. *Library Quarterly, 76*(2), 149-68.

Putman, H., Hansen, M., Walsh, K., & Quintero, D. (2016). *High hopes and harsh realities: The real challenges to building a diverse workforce* [Report]. Brown Center on Education Policy at Brookings, The Brookings Institution. https://www.brookings.edu/wp-content/uploads/2016/08/browncenter_20160818_teacherdiversityreportpr_hansen.pdf.

Rosa, K., & Henke, K. (2017). *2017 ALA demographic study*. ALA Office for Research and Statistics. https://www.ala.org/tools/sites/ala.org.tools/files/content/Draft percent20of percent20Member percent20Demographics percent20Survey percent2001-11-2017.pdf.

Index

readers' advisory: expertise and, 100–101; LIS education and, 138; picture books and, 19–23; popular culture and, 7

Readers' Guide to Periodical Literature (RGPL), 127–28

refugee youth, 28–29

relationships: authenticity and, 111, 113; interdepartmental, 33, 55, 133–34; with managers, 111, 116–17; with teens, 42, 55, 100

relevance, of library space, 36

representation, 36–37, 89–92; book challenges and, 70–71; in outreach, 27

research, 3–4, 155; empathy and, 139–40; expertise and, 139, 142; for publication, 138–39

research methods, in LIS curriculum, 53, 55–56

resistance, to teen spaces, 133–34

resources, 41, 46, 48; book challenges and, 65; for evaluation, 54; LGBTQIA+ services and, 90, 92–93

responsiveness, 3; services and, 131, 145

RGPL. See Readers' Guide to Periodical Literature

Rosenblatt, Louise, 98

safe space: discrimination and, 48–49; for LGBTQIA+ teens, 89–90, 94; libraries as, 40, 45–46

Sala, George A., 5

San Antonio Public Library, 11–12, 17

school librarians, 19, 22–23; LGBTQIA+ teens and, 92–93; selection and, 66

school libraries: book challenges and, 59–60, 62–63; education for, 159–63; history of, 126–29; self-censorship and, 70

self-censorship, 69; collection development and, 60; trust and, 70–72

self-definition, of teens, 101

self-knowledge, of librarians, 115–16

Senior High School Library Catalog (SHSLC), 126–27

services, 19, 143; challenges and, 149; collaboration and, 146; for LGBTQIA+ teens, 89–94; outreach, 25–28, 30–33; quantification of, 51–52; responsiveness and, 131, 145; youth-centered, 45–49. *See also* programs

SHSLC. See Senior High School Library Catalog

signage, inclusion and, 89

social action, librarians and, 83–87

social capital, of teens, 154

social control: adolescent development and, 76; built environment and, 78–79; teens and, 75, 77

socialization, 75, 89–90

social justice, 36–37, 161

social media: book reviews and, 7, 9n1, 21–23; communication and, 19–20; curriculum for, 20–23; misinformation and, 82–83; popular culture and, 6–9; teens and, 13–14, 106–7

social services: external resources and, 41; job titles and, 40; librarians and, 39, 100–101; outreach and, 28–29

social workers, 40; benefits of, 41–42; budgets and, 42; in public library, 39

solutions, challenges and, 112

specialization, age segregation and, 150–53, 155

staff, 153; Discord and, 16–17; openness of, 112; outreach and, 30–31; programming and, 154; teens and, 31, 156

stakeholders, transparency with, 135

status quo, opportunities and, 106–7

stereotypes, 37, 48, 91, 107, 144

Stevens, Rick, 63

Storey, John, 4

strategic plans, 157; outreach and, 32–33

strengths, organizational, 116

Stroshane, Eric, 60

success, 112, 116, 134, 141–42; cocreation and, 14–16, 46

summer reading programs, 52

super supporters, of libraries, 123

support, 123–24; book challenges and, 91; from communities, 64–65; from management, 54; of teens, 89–90

systemic barriers, 126–29

About the Editors

Anthony Bernier is professor at the nation's largest library school, California's San Jose State University School of Information, where he created and teaches the introduction to young adult services course every term as well as an annual course in youth services research methods. As a critical youth studies scholar, his primary research focus explores the administration of equitable library services with young adults.

Dr. Bernier published a regular column for *Voice of Youth Advocates* (between 2013 and 2019, "YA Strike Zone") in addition to his research appearing in many top scholarly journals. His most recent publications include *Transforming Young Adult Services, Second Edition* (ALA Editions, 2020), and "Isn't It Time for Youth Services Instruction to Grow Up? Superstition or Scholarship," *Journal of Education for Library and Information Science* 60(2), 118–38.

He has been awarded two National Leadership Grants from the Institute of Museum and Library Services (IMLS) and grants from the American Library Association (ALA) and the Association for Library and Information Sciences Education (ALISE). He regularly consults with several architecture firms on young adult library spaces. The iSchool has awarded him Distinguished Service, Outstanding Professor, and Outstanding Researcher Awards. He has served as chair of the iSchool's Youth Services Program Advisory Committee since 2016.

As a practicing young adult specialist librarian and administrator for 14 years, he designed and executed the first purpose-built library space with teenaged youth (Los Angeles Public Library's acclaimed Teen'Scape Department) and served as the first director of young adult services for the Oakland Public Library. He also served a four-year presidential appointment to the ALA Committee on Accreditation and has chaired several national professional and academic associations (including two elected terms as chair of ALA's Library History Round Table).

Shari Lee is associate professor at St. John's University (SJU), Division of Library and Information Science (DLIS). She holds an MLS with a concentration in children's services as well as an Advanced Certificate in School Library Media. Dr. Lee is the Youth Services Program Coordinator and Advisor at SJU/DLIS, a position she has held since 2010. She also served as the School Library Media Program Coordinator and Advisor from 2011 through 2017, and as Convener of the DLIS Youth Services and School Library Media Advisory Board from 2011 to 2017. Dr. Lee currently sits on the Editorial Board of *Education for Information*.

Dr. Lee's research considers the changing notions and physical structures of the public library as place and space. She is primarily concerned with how architecture and design elements affect human behavior and how this applies to the public library setting—specifically teen spaces. This was the focus of her dissertation, *Teen Space: Designed for Whom?*, for which she received the 2011 Eugene Garfield/ALISE Doctoral Dissertation Award.

This notion of social control in the built environment was further explored for its utility in creating authentic teen spaces in a course Dr. Lee designed and has been teaching for the past 10 years. As such, she is an often sought out speaker and consultant on teen space design and use. Dr. Lee teaches seven other youth services courses, including Popular Culture and Young Adults, a course that she also designed.

In 2020, because of her background in LIS and research on teens, Dr. Lee was invited to collaborate with the Resilient American Communities (RAC) COVID-19 Initiative. RAC's data collection, communication resources, and collaborative community-building methods are intended to help communities respond to COVID-19 and its life-altering syndemic impact, with a specific focus on the most vulnerable—including teens. Dr. Lee was one of the facilitators of the RAC Serious Game Working Group: Simulated Solutions, a large-scale online multiplayer game designed to engage youth and community leaders in identifying strategies to address local concerns related to both COVID-19 and climate change in Bay County, Florida.

In 2015, Dr. Lee received the Young Adult Library Services Association Writing Award for the best article in *The Journal of Research on Libraries and Young Adults* (JRLYA). The article, "Beyond Books, Nooks, and Dirty Looks: The History and Evolution of Library Services to Teens" has since been deemed required reading in many youth services courses across the nation. She was the recipient of the ALISE/Norman Horrocks Leadership Award in 2014 as well as the 2023 ALISE Excellence in Teaching Award.

About the Contributors

Denise E. Agosto is professor in the College of Computing & Informatics at Drexel University, where she serves as director of the Master of Science in Information program. Her research investigates young people's use of information and information technologies, the role of social context in shaping youths' information practices, and public library services. She is widely published in these areas and is the recipient of numerous teaching and research awards. Most recently, she is the recipient of a 2022–2023 Fulbright Scholar Award, for which she spent six months conducting research into college students' experiences with misinformation at the School of Information Science, Federal University of Minas Gerais, in Belo Horizonte, Brazil.

Jackie Biger is associate professor of instruction for the School of Library and Information Science at the University of Iowa. With her background and specialization in school libraries, she is the coordinator for the Teacher Librarian Program. She has both her master's in library science and her master's in teaching. Jackie is a cofacilitator of the statewide Iowa Teacher Librarian Leadership Team. Her interests include advocating for the integration of high-quality literature in classrooms, designing library curriculum and standards with vertical articulation, and creating library experiences that are responsive to the needs of patrons and learners. Her professional experiences include public library and school library positions with service to children and teens. Jackie was head of youth services in Amherst, New Hampshire, and held positions as teacher librarian in both high school and elementary school settings within the state of Iowa.

Beth Brendler is associate teaching professor in the iSchool at the University of Missouri. Her areas of interest include the sociocultural aspects of literacy, inclusive library services to diverse and underserved populations, and the socialization of children and adolescents through literature and media. Her research has examined rural school libraries as resources of community mental health literacy, library collections and services for LGBTQ* children and adolescents, intersectionality in self-published LGBTQ* e-book fiction, gender and literary response, identity and classroom book discussion, children's and adolescent literature about marginalized populations, gender construction in children's and adolescent literature, and socioeconomic status and literacy. She was the recipient of the 2021 ALISE Excellence in Teaching Award and the 2021 University of Missouri Golden Apple Teaching Award. She and her team also received the YALSA award for best article in *The Journal of Research on Libraries and Young Adults* in 2018.

Michael Cart, columnist and reviewer for the American Library Association's *Booklist* magazine, is the author or editor of 27 books, including his critical history of young adult literature *From Romance to Realism* and the coming-of-age novel *My Father's Scar*, an ALA Best Book for Young Adults. Prior to his relocation to the Midwest, he taught young adult literature at UCLA and the history of children's book illustration at Texas Woman's University. He is a past president of both the Young Adult Library Services Association (YALSA) and ALAN (Assembly on Literature for Adolescents of the National Council of Teachers of English). The recipient of the 2019 ALAN Award, he is also the 2000 recipient of the Grolier Foundation Award and the first recipient of the YALSA/Greenwood Press Distinguished Service Award. He lives in Columbus, Indiana.

Renate Chancellor is associate professor and associate dean for Diversity, Equity, Inclusion, and Accessibility at the School of Information Studies at Syracuse University. She received her master's and PhD in information studies from UCLA. Dr. Chancellor is an affiliated faculty at the Syracuse Lender Center for Social Justice. She has published broadly in the areas of critical cultural information studies, equity, diversity and inclusion (EDI), and social justice in library and information studies. She serves on the editorial boards of *Library Quarterly* and *Education for Information*. She also serves on the American Library Association's Publishing Committee. Dr. Chancellor received the Association for Library and Information Science Education (ALISE) Excellence in Teaching Award in 2014 and was recipient of the ALISE Norman Horrocks Leadership Award in 2012.

Anthony Chow is full professor and the director of the School of Information at San Jose State University. He holds a PhD in instructional design and an MS in educational psychology with a focus on systems design, human performance, and cognitive psychology. Dr. Chow's commitment to libraries resides in their role as anchor institutions for any organization or community they serve, especially in providing equity of access to free and high-quality information and resources for everyone. Dr. Chow is also the founder of Reading Nation Waterfall, which is an IMLS grant working with Native American children and families to increase access to reading materials and libraries. He is also a board of director and vice chair for the global Little Free Library organization and is a strong library advocate. He is married to his high school sweetheart and has three children.

Shannon Crooks is a candidate in the information science and technology PhD program at Syracuse University. She holds a bachelor's degree in social work from Winthrop University and a master's degree in social work from Howard University. Shannon earned her master's degree in library and information science from Syracuse University in 2018. Prior to joining the PhD program, she served as a librarian supervisor at an urban library in Prince George's County, Maryland. Shannon's background in social work enriches her perspective on library services and forms the foundation for her research on community engagement.

Roger B. Pereira Domingues is a librarian and master's student in the graduate program at the School of Information Science, Federal University of Minas Gerais, in Belo Horizonte, Brazil, where he recently taught as a trainee professor in the subject "Political Aspects of Disinformation." He is currently developing research that investigates how young people from public schools perceive what is disinformation as a way of understanding how the phenomenon of disinformation can be challenged in the scholarly environment.

Melissa Gross is professor in the School of Information at Florida State University. She holds a PhD in information science from the University of California, Los Angeles. She has published extensively in a variety of peer-reviewed journals, including *Library & Information Science Research*, *College & Research Libraries*, *Library Quarterly*, and the *Journal of the Association for Information Science & Technology*. Dr. Gross is a past president of the Association for Library and Information Science and the recipient of numerous awards for her research, teaching, and professional service. These include the prestigious American Association of University Women Recognition Award for Emerging Scholars in 2001, the 2019 ALISE Award for Professional Contribution to Library & Information Science Education, the 2020 Florida State University College of Communication & Information Graduate Faculty Research Award, and the ALISE 2021 best paper award (with co-author Don Latham). In addition, she has been the recipient of several research grants. Recent research topics include information-seeking behavior, information literacy, social services in libraries, and cyber defense as a collective activity system.

Mary Ann Harlan began her career in education as a middle school English teacher. She quickly discovered that she preferred to be in the school library. She earned her master's in library and information science from San Jose State University in 1999. In 2008 she returned to school to earn her PhD through the Queensland University of Technology/San Jose State Gateway PhD program. She began as a lecturer at San Jose State and was the program coordinator of the teacher librarian program. She is currently an associate professor at SJSU's iSchool. Dr. Harlan focuses research on information and reading practices and pursues how fiction functions as a source of information.

Ken Haycock is professor emeritus at the University of British Columbia and San Jose State University and currently research professor at the University of Southern California. Honored by many provincial, state, national, and international library associations, Dr. Haycock is an award-winning author and researcher currently focusing on governance as leadership and influence in organizations and politics.

Kafi D. Kumasi (she/her/hers) is professor in the School of Information Sciences (SIS). She is a leader in research on critical youth literacy and libraries. Her scholarship engages critical theoretical explorations of the intersections of culture, race, and schooling as a means to help prepare future and practicing library and information science professionals to meet the needs of all learners. Her work has been funded by the Institute of Museum and Library Services and recognized by the National Center for Institutional Diversity (NCID). Kumasi received her bachelor's degree in education from University of Michigan, Ann Arbor; her MLIS degree from Wayne State University; and her PhD from Indiana University, Bloomington.

Mike A. Males worked with youth in community and wilderness programs for 12 years; received a PhD in social ecology from the University of California, Irvine, in 1999; taught sociology, epidemiology, and psychology at the University of California for six years; authored four books and scores of journal articles and op-eds on youth issues; and currently is senior researcher for the Center on Juvenile and Criminal Justice, San Francisco (https://www.cjcj.org) and content director for YouthFacts (https://www.YouthFacts.org). He currently lives in Auburn, California.

Jamie Campbell Naidoo, PhD, is the Foster-EBSCO professor and unit head director at the University of Alabama School of Library and Information Studies. A former children's and school librarian, he researches and teaches in the area of cultural diversity in children's literature and librarianship. He is actively involved in the Association for Library Service to Children and the United States Board on Books for Young People. More about Dr. Naidoo is available at http://jcnaidoo.people.ua.edu/.

Gwendolyn Nixon is a doctoral student in the University of Alabama College of Communication and Information Sciences, focusing on library and information science, specifically school libraries and youth literature. She holds a Virginia teaching license with an endorsement in Library Media PreK–12 and is department chair and high school librarian in the Washington, DC, area.

Julia Burns Petrella is a doctoral candidate in the School of Information Sciences at the University of Illinois Urbana-Champaign and works as an instruction librarian at Dominican University. Julia received a bachelor's degree in psychology and a master's degree in library and information science from the University of Illinois. With a background in youth services librarianship, Julia has professional experience in public libraries and K–12 schools. Her dissertation research focuses on the ways that school library preparation programs teach future librarians about race, racism, and whiteness.

Jennifer Burek Pierce is professor in the School of Library and Information Science at the University of Iowa, jointly appointed in the University of Iowa Center for the Book. Her books include *Sex, Brains, and Video Games*, 2nd ed. (2017), *What Adolescents Ought to Know* (2011), and *Narratives, Nerdfighters, and New Media* (2020). *Narratives, Nerdfighters, and New Media* has been praised by John Green and *The Lion and the Unicorn*, which called it "an important book . . . drawing attention to a significant we-are-living-through-it shift in the history of reading." She has been awarded research fellowships at the American Antiquarian Society; Winterthur Museum, Library, and Gardens; and De Grummond Children's Literature Collection at the University of Southern Mississippi. Her research has won the Donald G. Davis Article Award and the Windsor Library History Essay Award from the Library History Round Table of the American Library Association.

Jolani Rhodenizer is an international librarian who has lived and worked outside of North America for over a decade with a focus on Arabian Gulf information environments. She is passionate about social justice in youth librarianship and how to foster empowerment and agency for young information seekers. She has written on the subject of power dynamics in information settings, cultural intelligence, and AI governance. She is currently the library manager at a Finnish international school in Qatar. She is delighted to be a part of the *Young Adult Library Services: Challenges and Opportunities* book project and to share her insights and experiences with fellow librarians.

Dina Schuldner earned her first master's degree in English language and literature at the University of Chicago. She earned a teaching certificate through a one-year graduate program at Queens College in Flushing, New York, and taught seventh-grade English and language arts for seven years. In 2010, she started her master's program in library science also at Queens College in Flushing, New York. Beginning as a part-time page in the Children's Department of Mineola Memorial Library in 2010, Dina had the opportunity to learn public libraries from the ground up. After 13 years in libraries, Dina has had the opportunity to serve as an adult reference librarian, a children's librarian, a young adult librarian, an academic librarian, a supervising librarian I, and now as a branch manager of the Little Creek Branch Library, a part of Norfolk Public Library in Norfolk, Virginia.

Jess Snow is the assistant manager of youth services for the Boston Public Library and has focused most of her work directly to and for underserved teens. She teaches an Outreach Services to Underserved Teens and Children to ALA and for San Jose State University. In 2020, she published a book, *Outreach Services to Underserved Teens: A Starter Guide*, through ALA Editions.

Patrick Sweeney is a tireless and innovative advocate for libraries. A graduate of San Jose State University's School of Information, he received *Library Journal*'s "Movers and Shakers" award in 2015 and was recognized with a "40 Under 40" award by the American Association of Political Consultants. He served as administrative librarian of the Sunnyvale (California) Public Library and is currently political director for EveryLibrary (the nation's first and only political action committee for libraries), where he works on political strategy for local, statewide, and national library campaigns and elections. Mr. Sweeney is co-author of *Winning Elections and Influencing Politicians for Library Funding* and *Before the Ballot: Building Support for Library Funding* and co-founder of the Think Tank. A sought-after speaker and presenter, he also teaches courses on politics and libraries at San Jose State University's School of Information. Mr. Sweeney can be found online as PC Sweeney.

Kerry Townsend is a PhD candidate at the University of Missouri with a focus on effective school libraries and youth services in public libraries. She holds graduate degrees in education technologies (MEd) and educational leadership and policy analysis (EdS) from the University of Missouri. Kerry previously worked as a high school English teacher, middle school librarian, and technology specialist. She now serves as the library media coordinator for Columbia Public Schools in Columbia, Missouri. Kerry works to help her school district and others support student and teacher learning through effective library media programs.

Jennifer Velásquez is the author of *Real-World Teen Services* (ALA Editions) and numerous articles on serving teens in the library setting. As an educational diplomat with the US Department of State, she has assisted libraries in the Czech Republic, Macedonia, Ukraine, France, and Italy with the implementation of services for teens. In 2011, *Library Journal* recognized her as a "Mover & Shaker" in the area of innovation, and she is the recipient of *The New York Times* Librarian Award (2005). Jennifer serves as coordinator of teen services for the San Antonio Public Library System (Texas) and is a lecturer at San Jose State University's iSchool (California).

Wayne A. Wiegand is often referred to as "the Dean of American library historians." He is the F. William Summers Professor of Library and Information Studies Emeritus at Florida State University. He is author of many scholarly articles and books, including *Irrepressible Reformer: A Biography of Melvil Dewey* (1996); *Part of Our Lives: A People's History of the American Public Library* (2015); and *American Public School Librarianship: A History* (2021). His next book, *In Silence or Indifference: Librarianship's Willful Blindness Toward Segregated Jim Crow Public School Libraries, 1954-1974*, will be published in September 2024. He is the former director of the Florida Book Awards and currently lives in Walnut Creek, California.